Pencil Pushers
Pencil Drawing A Beginner's Guide

LEGAL NOTICE

The Publisher has shrived to be as accurate and complete as possible in the creation of this report, notwithstanding the fact that he does not warrant or represent at any time that the contents within are accurate due to the rapidly changing nature of the Internet.

While all attempts have been made to verify information provided in this publication, the Publisher assumes no responsibility for errors, omissions, or contrary interpretation of the subject matter herein. Any perceived slights of specific persons, peoples, or organizations are unintentional.

In practical advice books, like anything else in life, there are no guarantees of income made. Readers are cautioned to reply on their own judgment about their individual circumstances to act accordingly.

This book is not intended for use as a source of legal, business, accounting or financial advice. All readers are advised to seek services of competent professionals in legal, business, accounting, and finance field.

To my Mom Richard and Muriel who supported me
All these years
Thank you
Ron

TABLE OF CONTENTS

INTRODUCTION
About this book
What it takes to be a Good Artist

HISTORY AND THE PENCIL
Where it all started
Evolution of the Pencil

TOOLS AN MATERIALS
Choose your weapon
Pencil, Eraser, Drawing Pad, Drawing Board, Paper stamps or Cone Blenders, Pencil Sharpeners, Rulers

BASIC DRAWING VS SKETCHING
Whats the difference
The Good, The Bad, How you should Hold the Pencil, Tripod Grip, Extended Grip, Underhand Grip, How to use Lines, Flat Lines, Contour Lines, Scumbling/Scribbling, Crosshatch Line, Smudge

PERSPECTIVE
Your point of view

Linear Perspective, Zero Point Perspective, One Point Perspective, Two Point Perspective, Three Point Perspective, Isometric Perspective, Atmospheric Perspective

WARMING UP
Let's do this

Kinds of Light Hard vs Soft Light, Hard Light, Soft Light, Cast Shadow, The Halftone, High Light or Full Light, Reflected Light, Artist Light, Shadows Light

SHADING
Drawing in the shade

Regular Shading, Irregular Shading, Directional Shading, How to Add Value, Some Tips on Tone and Value, Examples of Shading

THE CRITIC
Your own worst enemy

How to Draw Faster

FINISHING TOUCHES
Put a bow on it

Practical Exercise #1, The Drill Sergeant, Head Proportions, Cartoon Techniques, Practice Exercise #2 The Bulldog

CONCLUSION
Pat yourself on the Back

INTRODUCTION
About this Book

What is drawing? Drawing is the technique of taking something that is observed or imagined from the mind and transcribing that onto a medium or surface. That medium or surface could be, canvas, digital form, a cave wall or even on the human body. The objective of this book is to help beginning artists to develop there basic drawing skills.

Drawing has been a comfort in my life. To be able to find a quiet place, put in my earbuds, listen to music and spend hours working on a drawing has brought me peace, harmony, and joy in my heart. Being an Army Combat Veteran, I have dealt with many tragic, stressful, heartbreaking and life changing events in my life. I found that of any other intervention or therapy, drawing has been the best source for me to cope with today's stress. It is my "Go To" form of relaxation, decompression, distraction and detachment from traumatic past events. It prepares and relaxes my mind for future endeavors.

Today, like many tasks in life, drawing requires practice consistency and a love for the craft. This book addresses the basic techniques and provides practical tips that many great artist have been using throughout history, such as proper hand position, basic shading and perspective.

This book gives instruction as well as real world advise on developing, maintaining and improving one's skills using short, step by step theory and practical application that beginning graphic artist can use and apply.
My wish is that this book can be used to inspire the novice artist, sparking imagination, thought, artistic development and creativity. Enjoy.

What it takes to be a Good Artist

You don't have to receive formal training, attend some prestigious school or receive advanced technical training. Many artist are self taught. I feel that being self taught allows for greater expression of self and one's artistic fire. However, it is important as an artist to learn the basics such as composition, foreground, background, color theory, and perspective. Know the greats such as Michelangelo, Leonardo, or Picasso. Study various genres such as mural painting, digital media, tattooing or even automotive airbrush. Don't confine yourself to one area. Extend your skill set and explore other freelance opportunities when you feel the time is right, develop your talent.

During my time as an artist, I found that some aspects for me became more restrictive. For example, I took a course in architectural drafting when I was in college and I found it to be very rigid and mechanical. There was no room for error, self expression or creativity. It was all numbers and about fitting those numbers all into a "box". Another example would be someone standing over your shoulder telling you to draw a perfect circle with a ruler. It became too stressful to me and that was not the path that I wanted to take as an artist.

We live in an imperfect world. Who's to say what is perfect or not, suffice to say, I wouldn't feel safe in a skyscraper that was drafted by a commercial artist, graphic designer, abstract artist or cartoonist (no offense). What separates a good artist from a great artist? There is no simple answer. What is great art? What statement is the artist trying to make with there work?

I believe that as an artist it begins with a vision, an insight to birth an idea. There is a persistence to test the limitations of one's imagination. An artist must have an eye for detail. **Fore to seek detail is to seek perfection.** The artist must have a thirst for never ending creativity, this creativity brings value or worthiness, they must have a drive for uniqueness, a oneness with the universe that cannot be duplicated, they must have a true love for there craft, sprinkled with a fire in ones soul for self expression. I believe this makes a great artist.

History and the Pencil Where it started

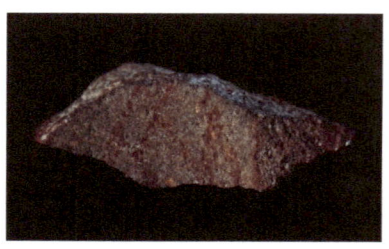

Drawing has been around since the beginning of mankind. The oldest known drawing dates back to 73,000 yrs ago. It was discovered on a rock in what is now the coast of South Africa. The drawing was on a 1.5 inch rock in what appeared to be a crisscross pattern of unknown meaning or origin. Archaeologist believed it to be left behind by humans that lived in the area between 100,000 and 70,000 years ago. Other known drawings date back to between 30,000 to 10,000 BC. These drawings were discovered on cave walls located in Spain and France.

Evolution of the Pencil

Around 3000 BC, Greek artist and scholars first used to draw and write on papyrus paper using metal stylus before the invention of the modern pencil. In history there are many famous artist in the world who preferred to use pencils. Vincent van Gogh, a notable artist, used Faber-Castell pencils to sketch his work. According to him, these pencils had superior quality. He liked its blackness and found it easy to use. Pablo Picasso used a pencil to create his works of art. Jean Auguste- Ingres made the Portrait of Mme Guillaume Guillon Lethiere.

John Constable created his works using a pencil and a sepia wash in his Trees and a Stretch of Water on the Stour.

These works, which were in part created with the pencil, are in various famous art galleries and museums around the world. In Cumbria England there were large deposits of graphite which locals used to mark sheep. The graphite, being a solid form, was wrapped in sheep skin making it more manageable as a marking tool. By 1662, England continued to produce these marking pencils. Italy was the first to use the process of splitting two halves of wood, inserting the graphite and re-gluing the halves.

During the Napoleonic Wars, France, unable to import graphite from England or Germany, forced Italy to invent something else. Nicholas Jacques Conte, an officer in Napoleons army, mixed powdered graphite with clay and burned it in a kiln in 1795. He created a mixture that could be used as a core of pencils by adjusting the clay to graphite ratio prior to the burning process. With this method, he could regulate the hardness or softness of the lead. This manufacturing process is still used globally today. Many years later the process became automated by Ebeneezer Wood and soon was mass produced by Joseph Dixon. Hymen Lipman perfected the process by attaching an eraser to the pencil. Today there are approximately 14 billion pencils produced annually. Pencils today have evolved into a variety of sizes, shapes, colors and types such as round shape, triangle, hexagonal, bendable, mechanical, or quadra chromatic.

Tools and Materials Choose your weapon

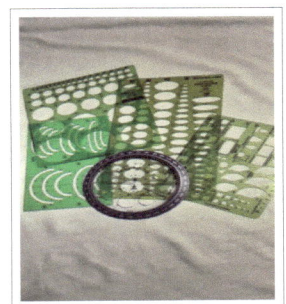

Materials and tools, choosing the right kind and quality, pencil, eraser, drawing pad, drawing board, paper stumps, cone blenders pencil sharpeners, ruler.

Don't sweat the small stuff. You can begin on a small budget. As I mentioned, pencil drawing doesn't require a lot of money. Its best to focus on skill rather than materials. Skill requires more time to develop and master than to have all the best tools money can buy at your finger tips. I don't believe money can buy talent, money can't replace true experience. With skill and time you can upgrade your materials which can make your craft easier and much more enjoyable such as purchasing a quality set of artist pencils, erasers, protractors ect..

think of it like this. It is more miserable to have no artistic skills with the best materials/tools available, than to have mediocre materials but have excellent artistic skills.

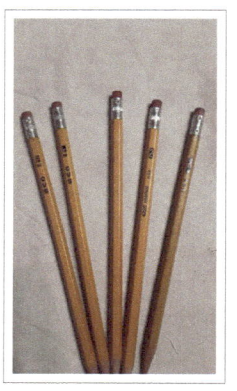
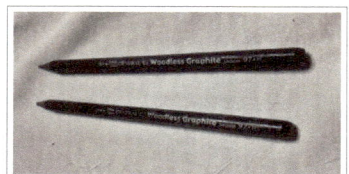
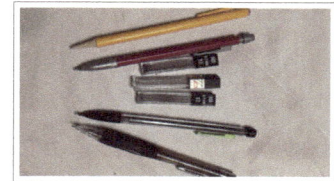
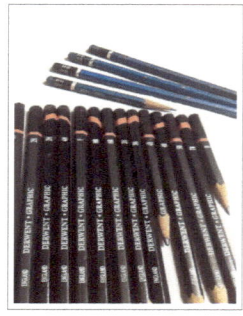

The Pencil

Pencils may vary depending on there purpose but generally the anatomy of the common # 2 wooden pencil consists of a graphite mixture encased in wood with an eraser attached. The artist pencil however can vary in hardness of the graphite making them extremely versatile. Manufactures use "H" for hardness, "B" for blackness "F" for fine point. (9B) being very soft to (9H) very hard. This variance in strength allows the artist a wide range of shading options. It helps the artist by allowing her/him to select the tone needed manually using the desired pencil and pencil hardness. The harder the graphite the lighter the tone. For users who cannot decide or wish to simplify things the #2 or HB pencil is the safest, most versatile choice, but requires one to be aware of the amount of pressure needed to make dark or light tones. With any wooden pencil, take care handling, dropping one may cause the lead inside to fracture. I can remember many occasions when I sharpened a wooden pencil down to the nub because the lead was broken, making it unusable. Mechanical pencils or technical pencils are another option. They can be useful for detailing work and are available in .5mm or .7mm. They require no sharpening and can be loaded manually with lead. The downside is that there is very little support for the lead and can be easily broken if too much pressure is applied.

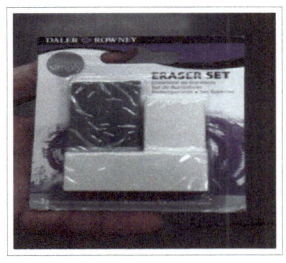 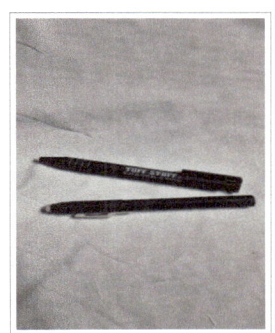 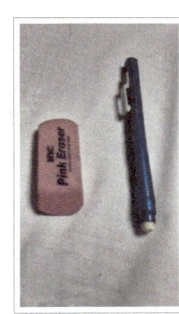

Eraser (leaving the past behind)

Being a beginner, you will more than likely burn though the pencils eraser before the pencil has been sharpen down. Because of this, a quality eraser is essential in an artist tool box. Erasers come from pulverized pumice. Use caution when using this type of eraser it can damage the paper. A less destructive choice is a soft vinyl eraser. It causes less damage and is good for more precise work and can effectively remove light marks. The kneaded eraser resembles chewing gum. Unlike the eraser made from pumice, this type of eraser does not leave any residue. Using your fingers, you can knead and shape this type of eraser to your desired shape making it easy to erase little details. This eraser is difficult to use in large areas.

An art gum eraser is yet another choice and is widely used among artist. Unlike the kneaded eraser, removing large areas is easier with this eraser. The downside of using a gum eraser is that it is not precise in erasing fine mistakes.

One thing I like to do is on a separate piece of paper is prep the eraser by removing any old residue as well as test it before use. This technique keeps you from grinding contaminates into your work. I Also find that some erasers may become brittle and dry with age making them unusable and harmful to your drawing. It's best to purchase fresh erasers from time to time to avoid eraser "smear" on your work.

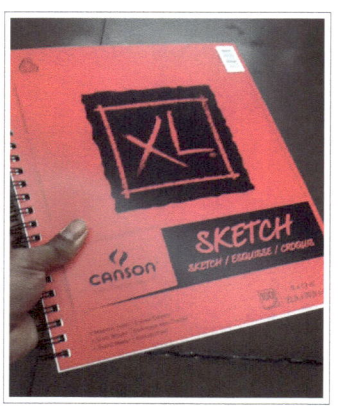 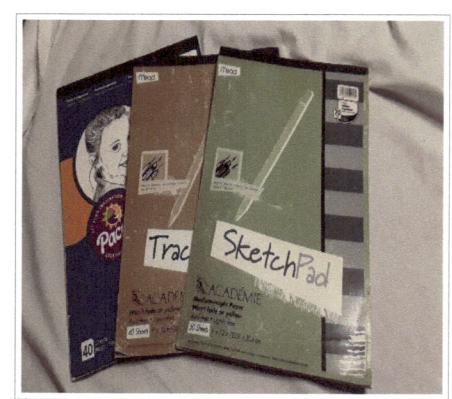

Drawing Pad

To compile your work consider purchasing a quality sketch pad. Sketch pads come in different sizes and types. Before purchasing consider what size suits your needs best, for example too large may be inconvenient or not allow maximum protection of your work from the elements if you choose to take it with you. Too small would not allow the artist to fully express there work properly. A spiral pad allows you to keep your work in place and organized. Portability allows the artist to experience the world up close rather than in a studio setting. Leonardo Da Vinci always had a sketch pad or a notebook with him. It allowed him to draw everyday objects and movement with ease. The artist pad can be broken down by texture or grade. Smooth paper is great for ink and graphite, while rough or toothed paper would be best for charcoal. The toothed texture allow the charcoal to grip the paper. When choosing your pad paper is also available in different thickness or weights. The thicker, the more expensive so keep this in mind. In addition, you should also considering purchasing some type of protector such as artists briefcase of vinyl case for your work.

The Drawing board

Comfort is king. Finding a good position which allows for maximum flexibility of your arms and movement is important, enter the drawing board. The drawing board places your work on a stable platform which contributes to giving your body, arms, wrist in a more suitable, supportive surface for drawing. Being able to draw without your work sliding is also important. One trick is to attach a clip to the pad and the board to give yourself more support and stabilization. This also keeps your paper from flipping back while you draw. Potato chip clips or something similar are an excellent solution.

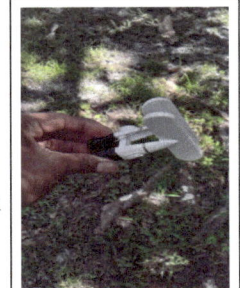

Paper Stumps or Cone Blenders

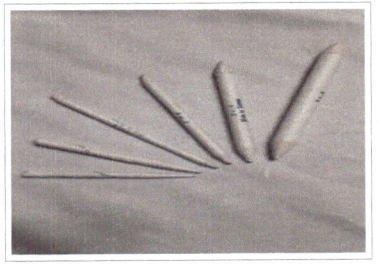

Blending is an essential part of drawing. Blending involves merging different tones so that they appear to flow naturally on the drawing. Blending Stumps or Tortillons are specifically designed to help. Do not use your fingers when blending. The human body produces oil which overtime can stain your work and become visible under certain light. The graphite on your hands can also smear your work which creates more issues. Remember keep your work clean and be aware of where you place your hands when handling your work.

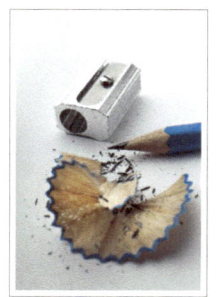 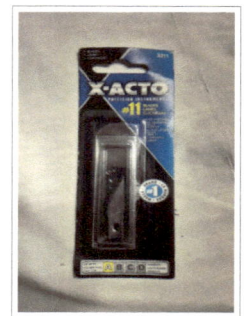 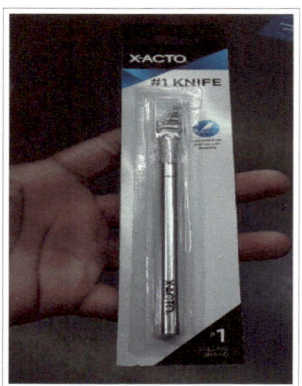

Pencil Sharpeners

A quality pencil sharpener can be an indispensable asset to your toolbox.
Pencil sharpeners can vary from a simple hand held device to high end, plug in electric models. You can use a
variety of tools to sharpen your pencil from x-acto knives to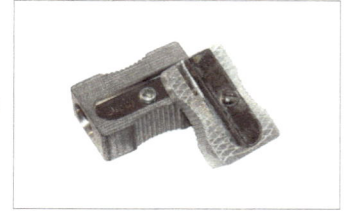
wooden sandpaper blocks. Understand, high end doesn't necessarily make it better. Sharpeners should be sharp and well maintained to allow you to produce quality work. Think of it like this, a lumber jack prepares his tools, (his ax), by putting a razor sharp edge on it prior to chopping down a tree. This allow the lumber jack to give maximum effort, use less energy, and get the job done quicker more efficient with better quality. This is a similar idea to having sharp pencil to work with.

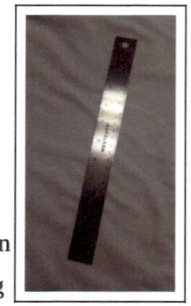

Rulers (rule)

   A ruler is used to finalize lines or shapes on your drawing. Since straight lines do not exist naturally, I find that a ruler or straight edge is mostly used on man made objects such as buildings, cars ect. I suggest, first lightly sketching out the straight line if possible. Use long strokes with a relaxed grip (hand and arm). When it appears straight, verify with the ruler then harden your line. For more technical effects it can be used to verify distances as well as symmetry between measurable points. Don't have ruler? remember a ruler is simply a straight edge. In the past when I was in a bind, I've used a credit card or the edge of a book as a substitute. This isn't always favorable, but it will work. Keep in mind, examine the item first, feel the edge to verify if it is truly straight (no nicks). I prefer a metal ruler. The reason is plastic bends contorts, and will crack and chip over time. Using a metal ruler allows your pencil to glide smoothly along the edge as well as a seamless transfer onto paper.

Basic Drawing vs. Sketching whats the difference
The Good the Bad and the Ugly of pencil drawing

The Good

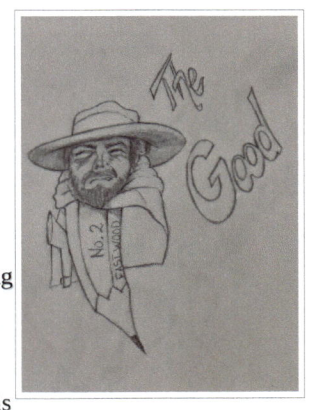

A few of the advantages of using a pencil as opposed to other writing tools are when an artist makes mistakes they can easily erase, if drawn light enough. This saves paper and time and aggravation. Being able to make on the spot corrections allows an artist to quickly adjust her/his work. These corrections can be compared to a sculptor chipping away at a rock until the desired result is reached, this is called sketching and creates a foundation for your work. Pencils are portable and easily available world wide as opposed to painting or using drafting equipment, which may require a more formal setting to render your work. There are various types of pencils and paper which we will discuss later. Due to this portability and being inexpensive, pencil drawing can be quite an enjoyable way to spend your time. Unlike painting, pencil drawing produces no toxic fumes, clean up is easy and requires no complex tools or special instructions.

The Bad

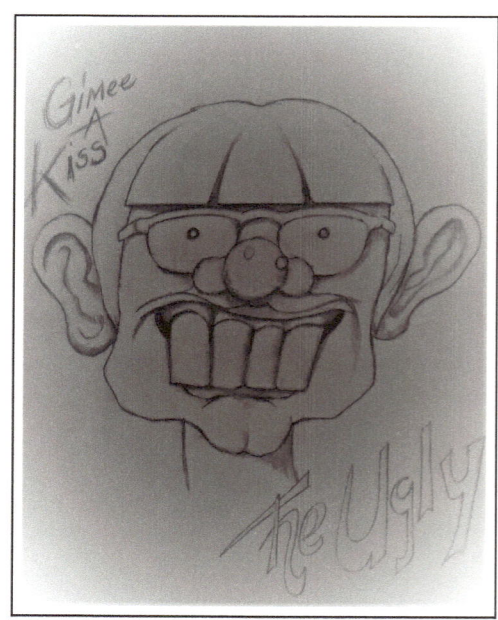

Pencil drawings will however easily smudge if you touch or rub them. It is important to pay attention to where you place your hands. It is a good idea to cover up part of your drawing with a clean cloth or separate sheet of paper to avoid unwanted smears or smudges. Wash your hand frequently to remove oils that our bodies naturally secrete or graphite that you may have accidentally picked up from your drawing. When you have completed your drawing it is a good idea to seal it using a quality fixative spray. You can also use hair spray that are perfume free.

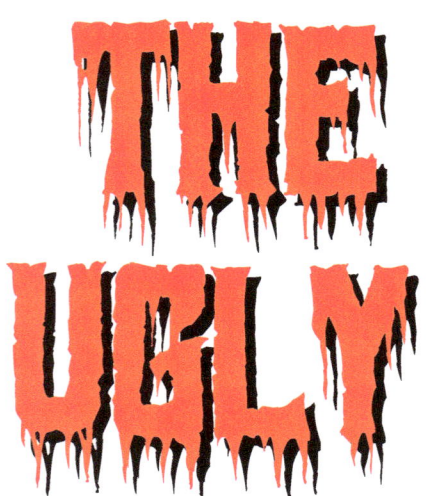

How should I Hold the Pencil?
The Different Pencil Grips

Tripod Grip

One of the most common ways to grip a pencil is the tripod method. This method is done by applying equal pressure between the sides of the middle finger, thumb and the tip of the index finger.
The pencil should remain flexible in your hand. Fine motor skills are required when drawing and these can be weakened if too much pressure is applied.
  Proper positioning is important. The index finger should be positioned on the tip of the pencil with the eraser generally pointed towards the shoulder.
  Proper positioning and grip allows you to draw effectively and maximize your motor skills. Proper positioning also reduces strain, fatigue and other potential physical problems such as carpal tunnel syndrome.

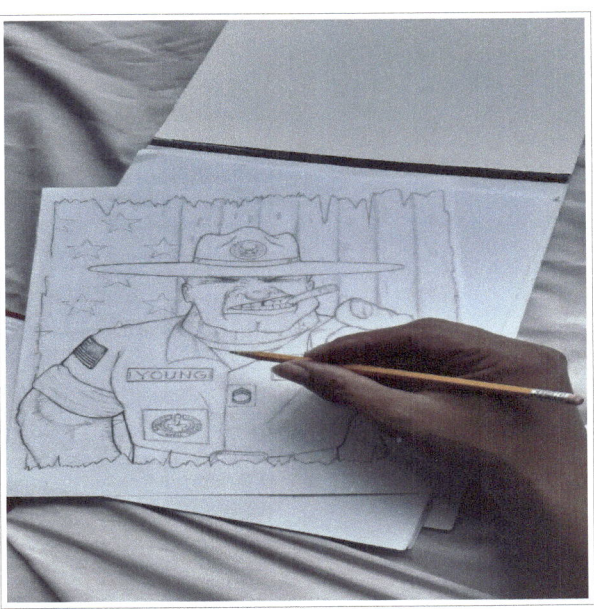

Extended Grip

The extended tripod grip is a variation of the tripod grip. The basic form that is used for the tripod grip remains the same. The major difference is the extended grip is now it will be further back towards the eraser. Because the hand is located closer to the end means that it will take shorter strokes to cover a larger area.

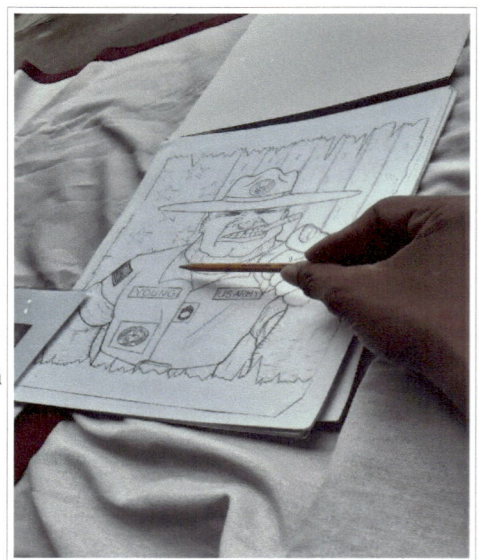

Overhand Grip

For sketching, many artists use the overhand grip. The idea of the overhand grip is to apply enough pressure relax your grip on the pencil but not so relaxed that control of the pencil is lost.

You can draw sitting or standing, just make sure that your arm has full range of motion. Shading is also easier with the overhand grip.

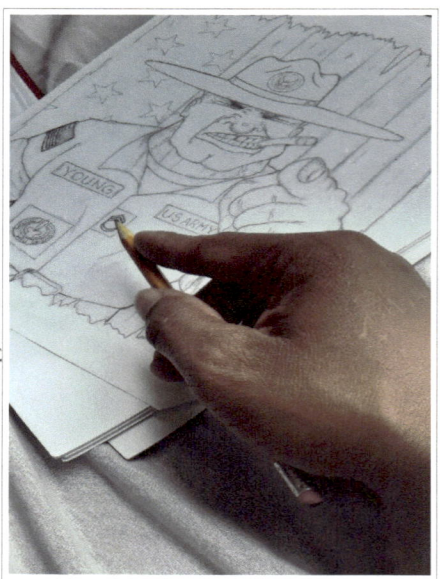

Underhand Grip

The underhand grip is another variation of the tripod grip. The pencil is held in a "V" position using the middle and the index finger controlling the movement. This grip is primarily used for broad sketching, firm lines and linear details.

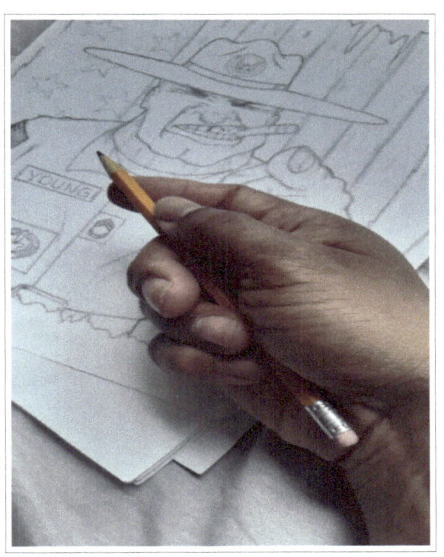

How to Draw Lines?

Straight lines do not exist in nature. What we see is man's visual interpretation of an objects edge. Lines in art are the artist guide or tool enabling him/her to break down what is visualized or imagined to create both space and image. Lines may vary depending on length, width value and in many other ways. When we think of form they can be straight jagged, curved or wavy. Line value can range from light to dark depending on the hardness of the graphite or the amount of pressure placed to draw these lines. These are basic lines used in pencil drawings. Feel free to practice drawing the objects below. Try to use the proper grip and pressure to get the right results, remember practice makes perfect.

Flat Lines

Flat lines or straight lines are commonly used to show or express an emotional response. It produces an illusion to the viewers eye. This can be done by sketching in a vertical, horizontal or diagonal direction depending on how or what effect the artist is trying to accomplish. Generally, a wider look can be produced using **Horizontal lines** as opposed to a **Vertical line,** producing a leaner, thinner look. In terms of emotions, vertical invokes poise and stillness. Horizontal lines involve serenity and stability. While **Diagonal lines** involve movement, unrest change instability and variation.

Accent Lines

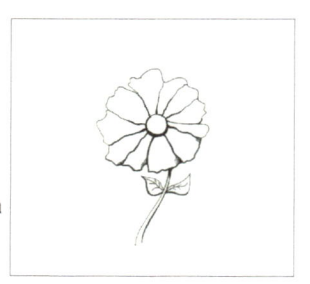

Accent lines are used to help your art stand out. For example, when we speak it is not in a monotone voice, we emphasize certain parts of speech to show emotion (high pitch, low pitch, pauses, inflection, ect.). Accent lines are similar, they make your art stand out. When pressure is applied to the pencil in certain areas, it emphasizes shadow or weight in the drawing. Accent lines point out or accent portions of your drawing. This is done by placing special stress on certain changes and variations in your lines.

Contour Lines

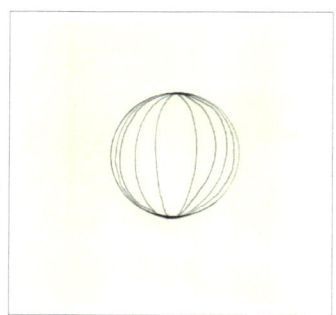

The beauty of contour lines is to enhance the contour and shape of an image. This striking characteristic is the purity of the line. In drawing and sketching the eye follows this important edge, it outline and contours the object you draw.

Scumble/Scribbling

Scribbling or Scumble is simply using random, abstract or squiggly lines to produce a shadow effect forming an object. This technique requires impulsiveness and a certain amount of looseness in the arm, wrist and hand.

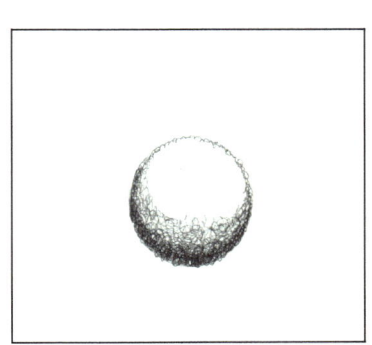

Cross Hatch Line

Cross hatch lines are often used in cartoon illustrations. This type of shading differentiates itself from other forms and is certainly useful in creating a shading effect.

Cross hatching is created by intersecting parallel lines to produce different densities of light or darkness. These shades can vary depending on the density or closeness of these crosshatched interlaced lines. An example of this can be seen in many comic strips, comic books, magazines, textures, and wall illustrations.

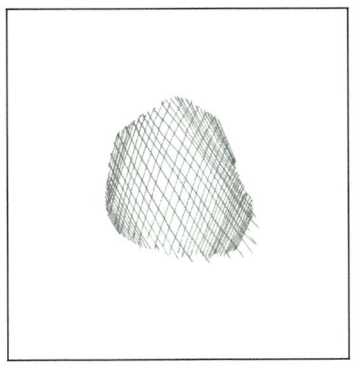

The application of crosshatching produces a flat image while the use of curved lines produces an illusion of plumpness and mass. Thus, two similar objects may have different illusions due to the use of lines.

Smudge

Smudging deals specifically with blending. Smudging simply is drawing an object and shading it using the kind of value you want it to have. It can then be blended properly using a tissue, cotton puffs or paper towels.

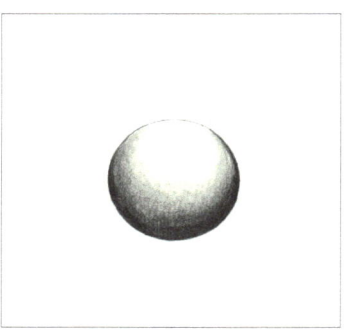

Pointillism

Pointillism is a technique of Neo impressionism Painting. It was developed by Georges Seurat in 1886. It was originally a term used by critics to describe, mock or ridicule certain works of art. Pointillism, also known as Stippling or Divisionism is a technique of grouping dots to create a shaded image. The idea is that the closer the pattern of dots are together the darker the drawing will be. Using this method the artist must first create the foreground before filling the inside.

Warning pointillism can be a very slow, tedious, and monotonous process so be patient.

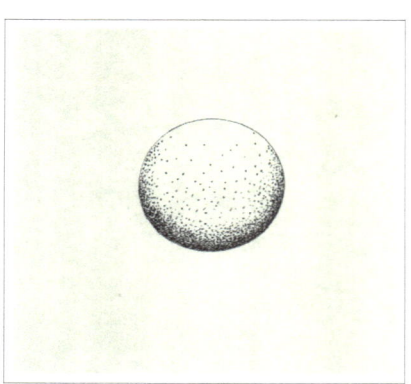

Perspective (your point of view)

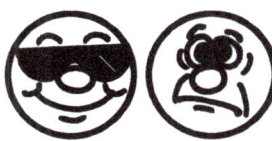

Perspective, when applied to your drawing, adds photo realism and depth. It allows the viewer to see objects and features in 3D on a 2D surface. There are 3 major types of perspective 1 point, 2 point and 3 point. Perspective gives your art form dimension, distance and a spacial realistic element. Perspective is one of the most basic elements discussed in an art course. One example of perspective is if you stand in the center of a railroad track looking along the line, the train tracks will appear to meet on the horizon. This is of course an optical illusion as well as an example of simple linear perspective. There are several types of perspective that we will look at.

Linear perspective

The theory behind this method is that the farther away an object is, the smaller it becomes. While the closer it is the larger it appears. When an imaginary line is drawn from the top and bottom of a subject, where they converge on the horizon line is called the vanishing point.

Zero Point Perspective

Zero point perspective is when there is no vanishing point. An example of this is a mountain range. There are no visible lines or apparent vanishing point to relate to as an anchor point, this is considered zero perspective, yet when observed the mountain will still appear to have the same observable depth.

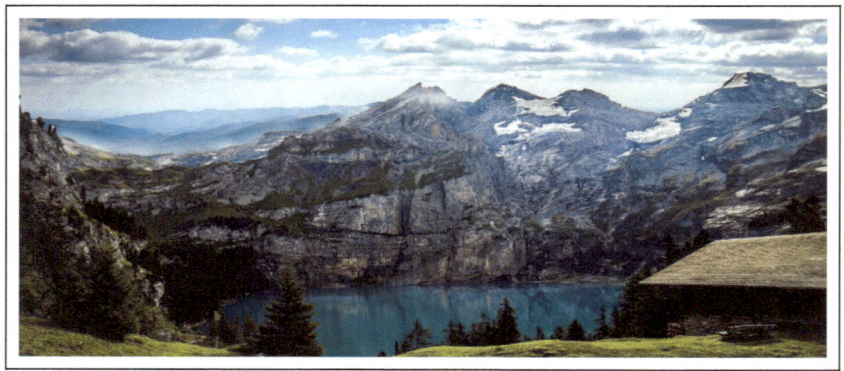

One Point Perspective

One point perspective is when there is only one vanishing point on the horizon line. This vanishing point directly faces the viewer, examples of this are rail road tracks, roads, buildings or hallways.

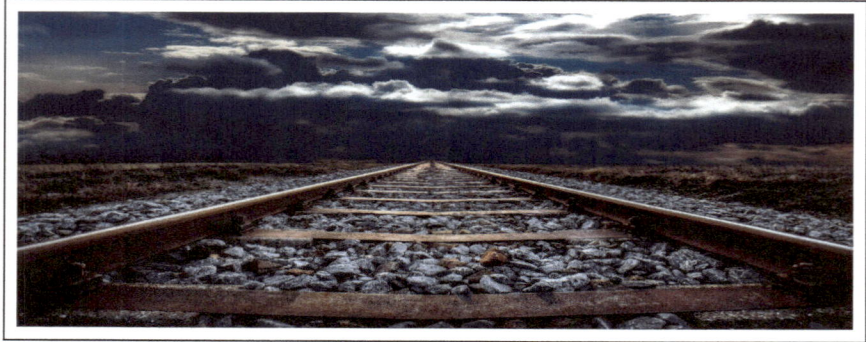

on the next page is an example of a drawing using one point perspective. Note: a ruler or straight edge may be helpful to keep your lines straight when attempting this type of drawing.

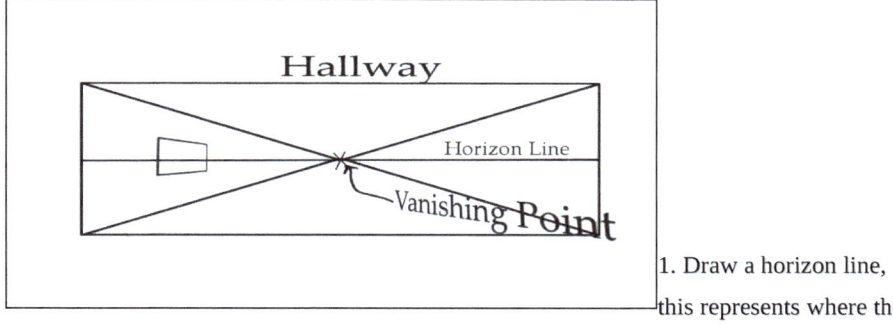

1. Draw a horizon line, this represents where the sky meets the earth.

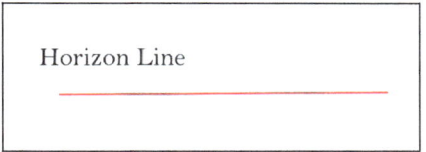

2. From your horizon line, select a vanishing point note: it can be in the center, close to the left or right of the drawing.

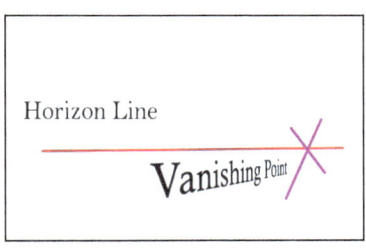

3. Lightly draw two lines from the vanishing point diagonally, the top lines should extend slightly past the bottom. Draw two vertical lines and connect the 2 horizontal lines, this will begin to form the side of the box.

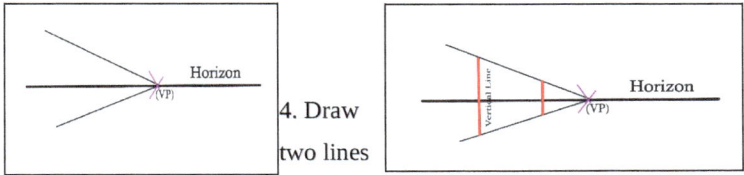

4. Draw two lines

parallel to the horizon line from the top and bottom line. This will help form the front of the box.

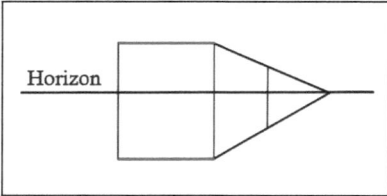

5. Connect and close the box by drawing a line from the top line to the bottom.

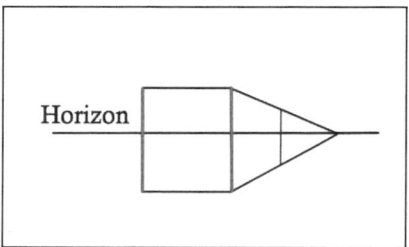

Finally clean up your work by erasing your guide lines that extended from the horizon as well as those inside the box. You can further enhance your drawing by shading, depending on your purpose.

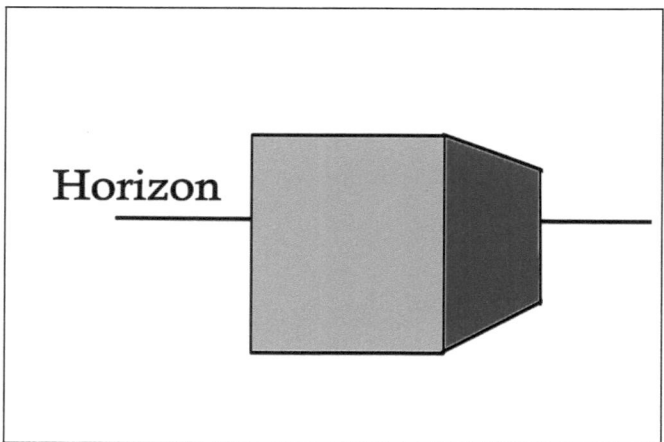

Two Point Perspective

1. Two point perspective involves having two vanishing points rather than one. To do this draw a horizon line as in one point perspective.

![Horizon Line diagram]

2. Instead of 1 point, mark 2 points on the right and left of the horizon line.

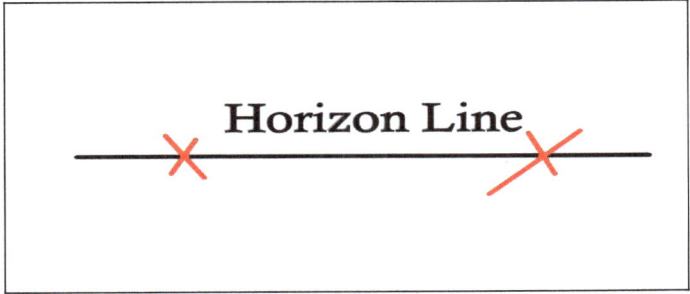

3. Lightly draw a construction grid consisting of six lines coming from each vanishing point and locate where the lines converge in the middle.

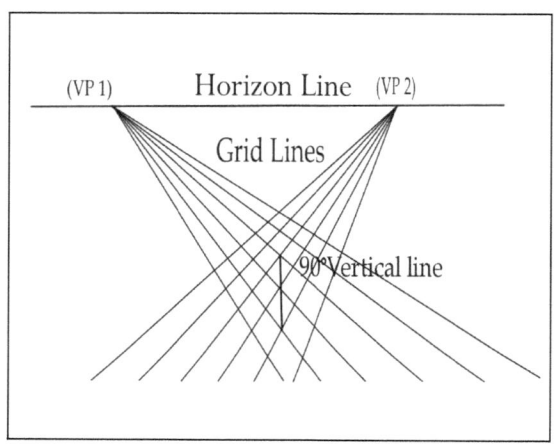

4. Draw lines at 90° from the horizon line this will form the corner of the box

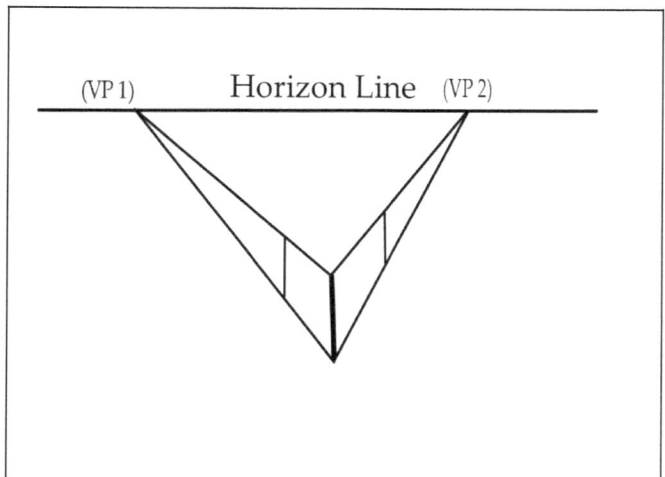

5. From the vanishing points, draw top and bottom lines to connect the vertical line to the vanishing points as guides, this should resemble a "V". This is the top and bottom edge of the box.

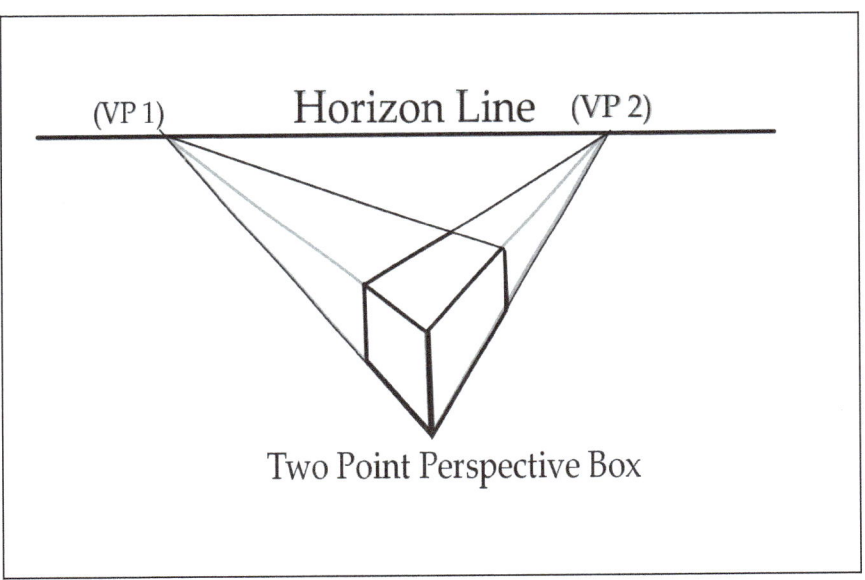

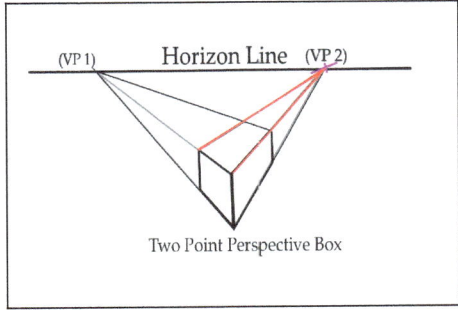

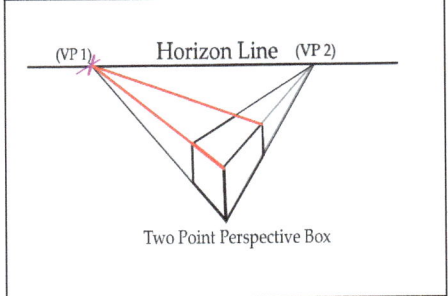

6. Draw 1 line to the left and right parallel of the original vertical line, these will determine the length and width of the box.

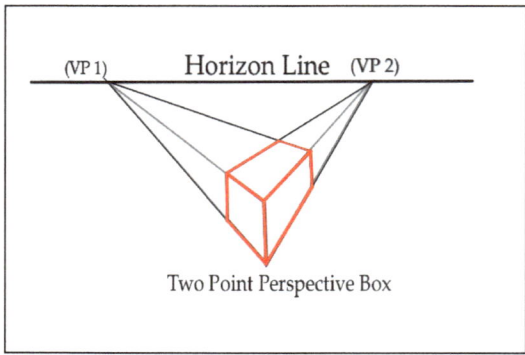

7. From the vanishing points draw the line connecting your right vanishing point to the left vertical line and your left vanishing point to the right vertical line, this will form the top of the box. Finally erase any guide lines and shade as needed.

Three Point Perspective

Three point perspective is commonly used in architectural drawings. Parallel lines along the width of an object meet at two separate points on the horizon and vertical lines on the object meet at a point on the perpendicular bisector of the horizontal line.

1. Begin by drawing a horizontal line as you would in 1 or 2 point perspective. Place your vanishing points (VP) as close to the edge as possible. The horizontal line in this case will be different.

Place it near the top of your paper if the viewer is looking down (**Birds Eye View**) if the viewer is looking up the line should be near the bottom (**Ants View**). In this case we will be working with Ants View.

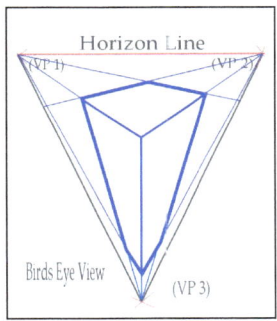 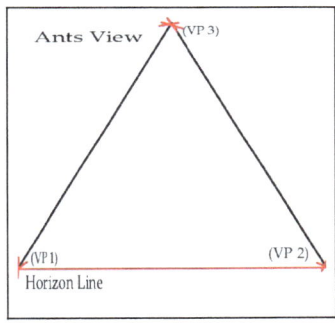

2. for Ants View position the 3rd (VP) as far from the horizon line as possible. Try to position it near the top center of the paper for a better effect. The triangle is important, it will serve as a "frame or guide" everything must fall within this guide.

3. Now lightly draw a line from your horizontal line to (VP) 3. you don't have to connect with it simply use it as a guide.

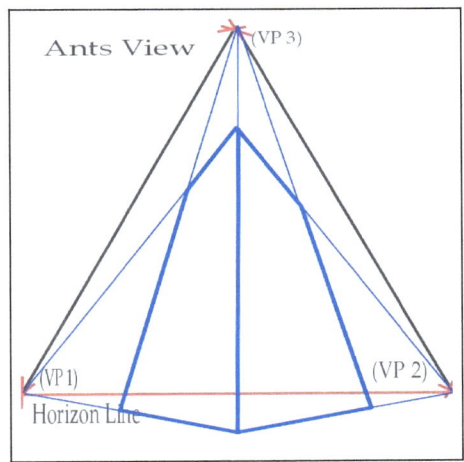

4. Next lightly draw lines from (VP) 1and 2 just as in 2 point perspective. This may serve as guides to the sides of your building.

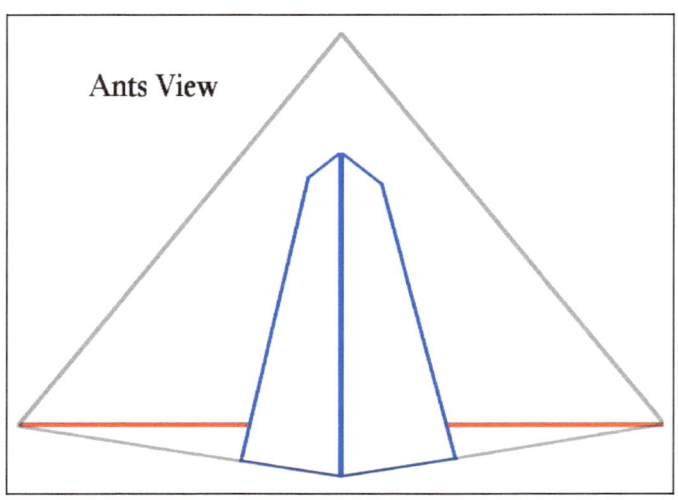

5. Determine where your building ends in space. Lightly draw lines from (VP) 3 through both sets of lines receding towards the two horizontal (VP)s.

6. Finally lightly draw lines from the back corners towards the opposing horizontal (VP)s. clean your work up by erasing any stray lines and shade as needed. Remember this is basic, with practice more detail can be incorporated building more complex features into the structure. Also reversing the placement of the horizon line can create the opposite effect and therefore a different view.

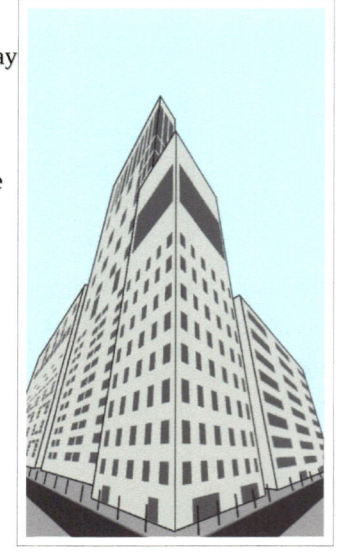

Isometric Perspective

Where 1and 2 point perspective have vanishing points, isometric perspective provides a view where there is no visible vanishing point. There is no point where multiple parallel line may converge. An example of this is a room or box as seen below.

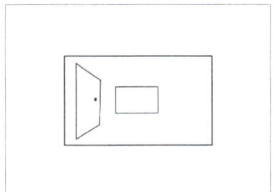 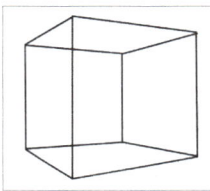

Atmospheric Perspective

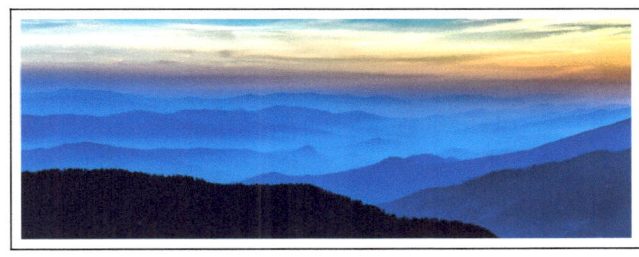

Atmospheric or aerial perspective creates the illusion of depth by modulation of tone or color making the subject appear to be distant. An example of this can be seen with the haze of distant mountains illustrating the contrast between foreground sharpness and background blur.

Warming up Let's do this

You should look at basic shapes as being the framework of your drawing as a beginner. When in doubt conceptualize by using the most basic shapes to get a rudimentary idea of how a subject is broken down. This takes imagination and a bit of finesse. For example the human head might be

visualized as an oval or circle, the arm as a cylinder. Start with basic shapes such as a square and imagine your subject, whatever that may be. Deconstruct the subject in order to build it back up. Understand that basic shapes have no volume but are the foundation for creating form, this is our goal. Basic shapes are 2 dimensional having (height and width) such as a square, circle or triangle. When we add volume (depth) we now have a cube, a sphere and cone. This 3D effect, with practice can be applied to produce photo realism in your work. Further shading can enhance this effect.
 Below are examples of shapes vs. volume

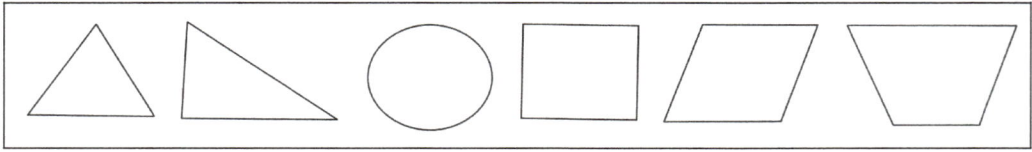

SHAPE

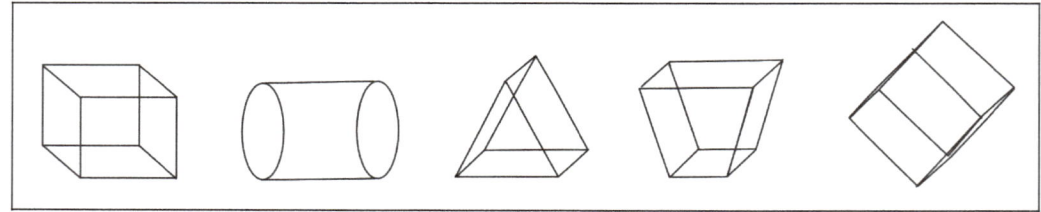

VOLUME

When drawing the human body you can use these basic shapes for eyes and faces, especially when drawing cartoons. Look at the drawings bellow. Know that we aren't all perfect and this can be evident through drawing. For example, look at the shapes of the human body. At different points in our life span our head, eyes the various hair styles differ and will change throughout our lives. As humans, no two of us are exactly alike, but yet we do all share some common, basic features as humans. These features can be mentally, visualized by deconstructing them into there most fundamental shapes.

Car closely following the basic outline

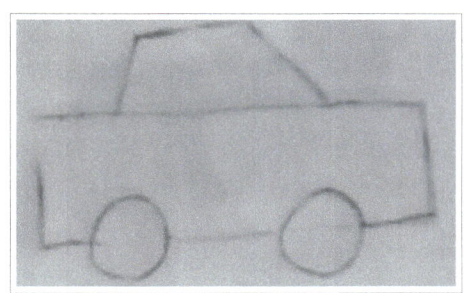

Car that did not follow the basic outline

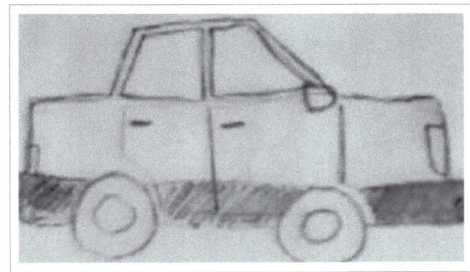

You can also use basic shapes for eyes and faces, especially with cartoons. Look at the drawings below.

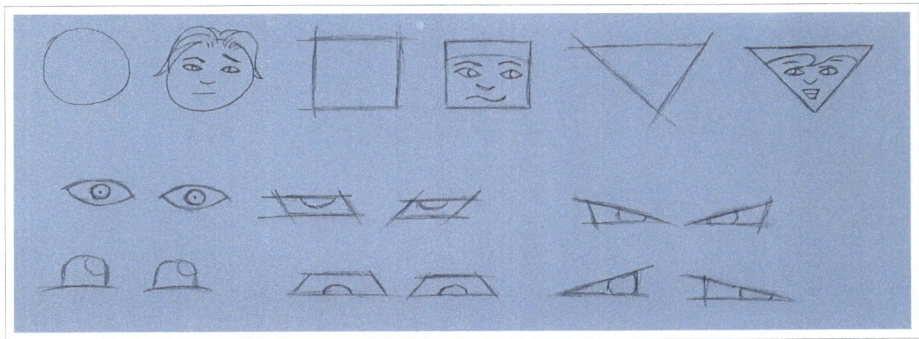

Kinds and Quality of Light (hard light vs soft light)

Hard Light

When it comes to light, be aware of the source. Among the sources of hard light are sunlight on a bright cloudless day, the standard camera flash, the naked bulb with clear glass ect. Hard light cast harsh shadows and draw attention to certain parts of the drawing. This is accomplished by applying direct light.

Soft light

Soft light is used to hide imperfections. This type of light is more subtle to create soft shadows. Regular household bulbs can be used to provide this effect.

The Cast Shadow

This refers to areas in your drawing that are the darkest and require more shading. Light maybe completely blocked or objects may cast a shadow obscuring light. With practice these areas will allow you to bring depth and a lifelike effect when used properly.

The Halftone

AKA Mid tones refers to the areas that boarder on dark and light, they retain a gray value. The mid tones reflect consistency in terms of an objects true tone or color.

Highlight or Fill Light

This is when light is directly on the subject, reflecting the brightest ares in your drawing

The Reflected Light

Light that is reflected on an object from a nearby source or surface.

Artist Light

Lighting on your pad also should be observed when rendering your art. Obviously without proper lighting you can't produce quality work. Proper lighting reduces eye strain and fatigue. Be aware of your choices of light sources and quality when drawing for long periods of time.

Shadows Edge

The area found between mid tone and reflected light

Shading (Drawing in the Shade)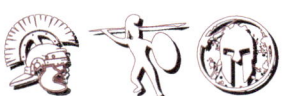

Regular Shading

Move the pencil horizontally or vertically to produce this shading technique. Vary your pencil pressure to lighten or darken.

Irregular Shading

The pencils direction changes in inconsistent, regular intervals. Circular motion or stroke is used to achieve this effect.

Directional Shading

Two directions are used to achieve this effect when using the directions, you should never overlap.

How to Add Tones and Values?

If we want create a more realistic 3D drawing it is important to pay attention to lighting and shadowing. We must first imagine where the light source should be and determine how and where the shadow will cast from this light source. When shading remember although a drawing may appear to be all black or white this is a mere illusion caused by contrasting parts of the drawing. These gray grades that appear between white and black are known as halftones.

Here is an illustration of a shaded pole from a certain source of light.

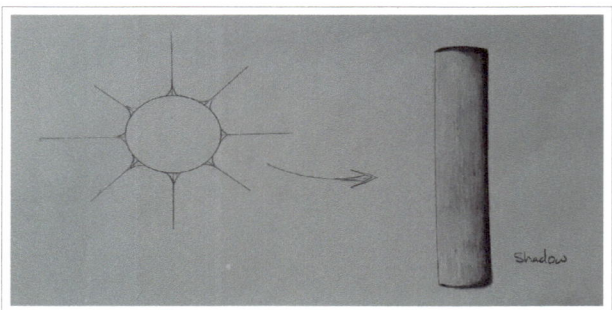

Below are computer-generated half tones. It is computer generated to let you see the clear distinctions between the shades.

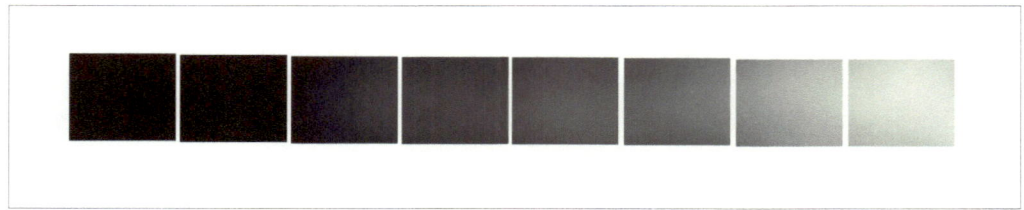

This rectangle is the result of combining these tones, a fluid shade. Halftones give the illusion of form and shape which transforms the drawing from a 2D image to 3D.

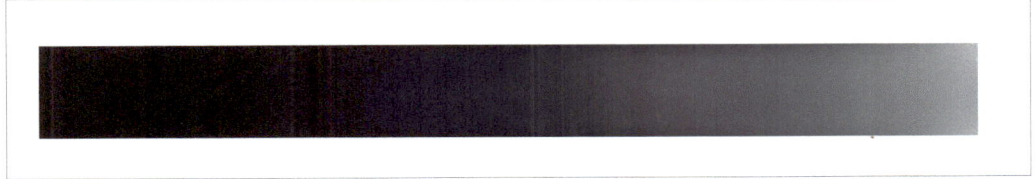

Some Tips on Tones and Values

In shading, B pencils will give you the best effect by adding depth to you drawings. Gradual pressure should be applied when shading to create a smooth even look. In shading, a blunt pencil is more effective than a sharp one. Your strokes should be near each other to maintain a consistent look. Form is created with variations of dark and light shades, this eliminates the need for hard outlines.

Some Examples on Shading

Unshaded Pepper

Shaded Pepper

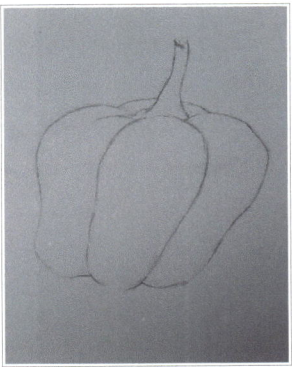
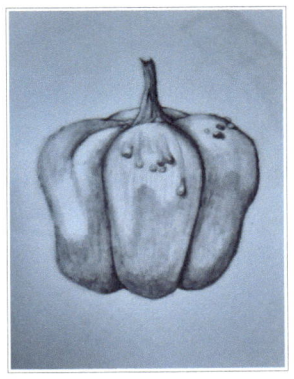

The Critic (YOUR WORSE NIGHTMARE)

What I mean by this heading is that you need to be your own worse critic when it comes to you drawing. As I mentioned building a solid foundation is important. It is a good idea to critically evaluate this prior to solidifying a final rendering. To do this there is a technique that I use. I simply walk away. It may seam strange, but this allows me to return with a fresh set of eyes and give the drawing a true, honest evaluation according to what I think I am trying to accomplish on paper. I try to periodically do this while I draw and is a continuously repetitive process. As time goes on I make fewer and fewer corrections to the drawing. In my minds eye its not what is right with the drawing, but the opposite what is wrong, what do I need to do to improve on my work, and how much effort do I want to put into it. This process may take several iterations, lasting minutes, hours or days. I have stepped away from a drawing for months and worked on another project to remove the artist block. I would then critique and reengaged with renewed concepts and inspiration. This process again can be compared to a sculptor. The ultimate goal is creation from ciaos, creating something out of nothingness into a thing of beauty. So what am I looking for when critiquing? Any and everything. For example, is a section too light or too dark, does the drawing look skewed to one side, is the symmetry off making one side appear too short, did I draw so hard that it left un-erasable marks embedded in the paper, is the shading off in some way, is the drawing not centered or the composition off, is something misspelled (yes this has happened to me). These, and many other problems should be addressed prior to picking up the pencil as well as be closely monitored throughout the process of creating your drawing. When sculpting your piece you can't un-chip the rock, so pay attention. Establish a solid foundation, build upon it constantly and consistently making adjustments. You will be the ultimate judge of your work, no one else!!! There will always be other artist who are better and worse. Know your place, and be comfortable in it. You know the work and effort you put into the piece, so be proud of your accomplishment even if those amateur critics don't agree.

How to Draw Faster, The need for speed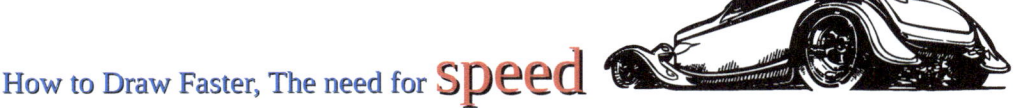

When you first start it should not take hours to complete a simple sketch. Drawing should be relaxed stress free and enjoyable. Pay attention to what you are doing and how you are doing it. If it's taking you hours, it's not the process, it's because you may be struggling with the basics. This is barring you from moving forward with your work. Like building a house it is important your frame is straight strong, with a solid foundation or your house will fall. Apply this analogy to your drawing.

Many artist can draw at lightning speed. The key to this is practice, practice, practice. First try timing yourself. Train your mind to get as much on paper as possible, even if it seams like gibberish or chicken scratch. Loosen your wrist and grip on the pencil. Allow your hand and arm to lightly flow onto the paper. Details during this timed exercise are not be important. The goal is quantity not quality at this point. Practice drawing drawing people or objects, start with basic shapes. Final details can be added later. Daily practice is important and will contribute to developing skill and quality in your work. Start with 30 seconds for the rough draft. Use a light pressure with long pencil strokes. Take your time with the details, which again can be added later. This speed sketch may seam like a hot mess at first but keep practicing and you will improve your technique.

Finishing Touches

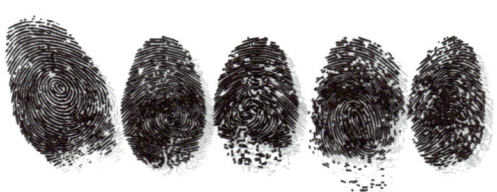

Are you finished? Not quite…

When you feel that you've done all you can and are satisfied with the results it's time for clean up. What you need to do first is go over the entire drawing, every inch. Remove any stray marks. Choose an eraser that suits the type of paper and task, whether small or large areas. While drawing, if you were careful not to use too much pressure on your work, clean up should be a breeze. When your finished erasing use a brush to remove residue from the drawing by tilting and shaking. Now your ready for the world to see and admire it.

Consider using a fixative to seal your drawing. A fixative is a liquid similar to varnish which is sprayed over a finished piece of artwork. Fixatives preserves your artwork it prevents smudging and smearing. Modern fixatives are usually alcohol based and hydrocarbon propelled. Here are a couple of example I completed years ago using some of the basic techniques from this book.

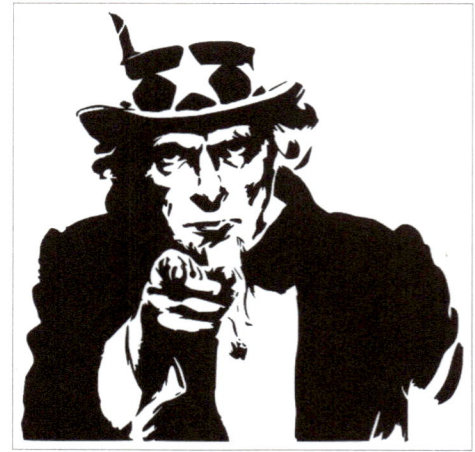

I WANT YOU TO PRACTICE

PRACTICE EXERCISE 1

THE DRILL SERGEANT

The idea for the Drill Sgt came from a poster of Uncle Sam. I wanted it to resemble an old recruitment poster. Being in the military, I remember how tough my Drill Sgt was, almost super human. I wanted this Drill to look cartoon-ish but tough as nails someone you didn't want to tangle with on a bad day.

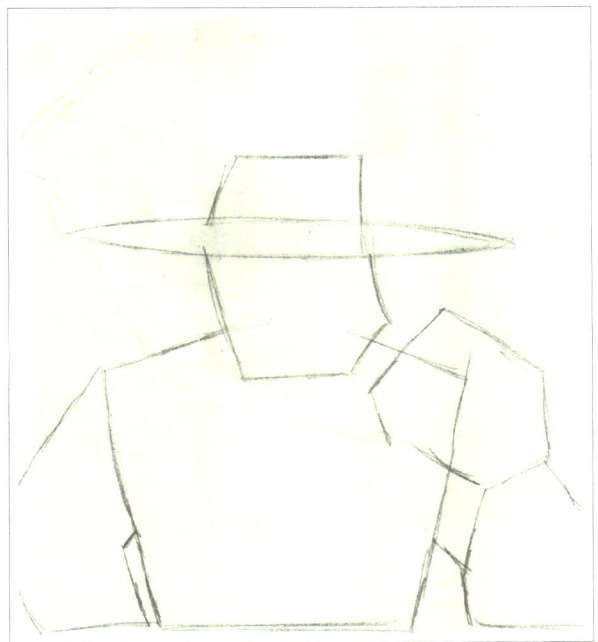

I decided I wanted to draw just from the torso up, this would emphasis his facial expressions.

1. First start with a sharp pencil, I suggest a #2HB mid grade. I began with basic shapes a loose break down of how I wanted the character to look. When beginning make sure everything is centered on your paper. Your drawing should not be so large that it

will extend past the perimeter of the paper or so small that it does not fill the paper fully. Draw a pentagon on the bottom half of your paper this will form the torso. Now the head, which is slightly tilted to the left with another smaller one angled to the right. Sketch out the brim of the hat drawing as a horizontal, tight oval. The eyes should be lightly sketched slightly below the brim of the hat as two horizontal lines for now. The nose is placed midway between the chin line and the brim of the hat. The mouth will be right angled triangle shaped and it is located halfway between the bottom of the nose and the top of the chin line. Vertically the eye placement should be broken down into 5ths (see diagram) the 2nd and 4th bracket will form the eyes (see diagram). Other features will be centered using a lightly drawn vertical line down the center of the head as a guide to maintain symmetry. (See head proportions)
-

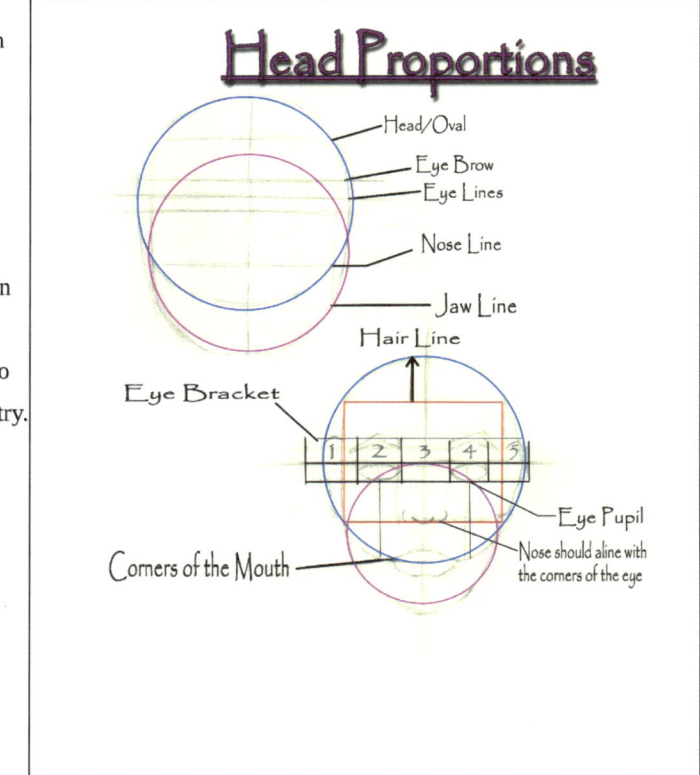

2. The left arm will resemble two "V"s connected to the torso. The right hand and arm are pentagon shaped. Remember sketch lightly in case you make mistakes and be patient. Tip; when I run into a bind and have issues trying visualizing how a pose will look, I sometimes take a selfie to orient myself jump starting what I'm trying to visualize and create. This is no different than using a model or a photograph for reference. Pencil pressure at this stage is important, the lighter you sketch the drawing, the better.

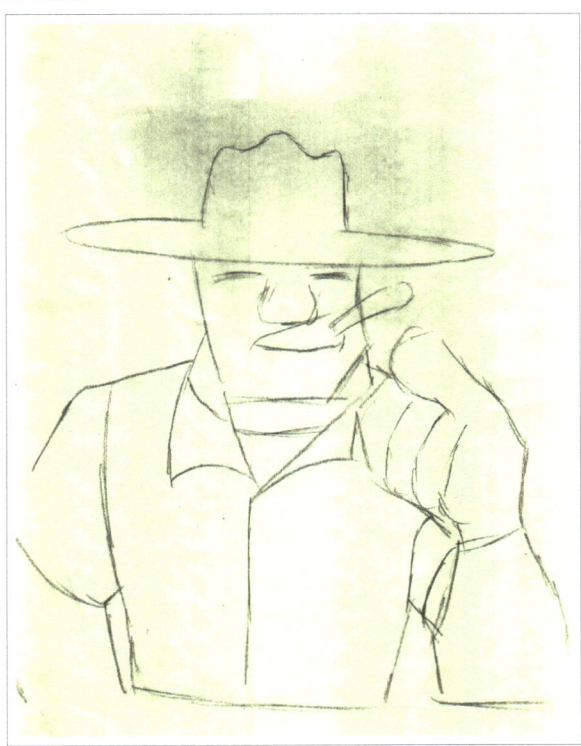

3. Next we begin to "carve" into our basic shapes. Keep in mind at this stage you should feel confident with your foundation. At this stage we can begin to build upon the foundation. From the top, draw a smooth "W" for the top of the DI's hat. Lightly sketch where the eyes may be placed. Draw below the brim of the hat. The eyes should resemble the shape of a football, again they should fall into the #2 and #4 brackets. Halfway between the brim of the hat and the bottom of the chin lightly draw the bottom of the mouth and form a right angle triangle as well as begin to sketch out where the teeth will be shaped. The teeth I decided would not be perfect just to give the DI more personality and uniqueness. One third of the distance from the bottom of the mouth and the brim of the hat is the bottom of the nose. The nose will be a circle and over sized with the nostrils extending to be roughly inline with where the pupils of eye would fall.

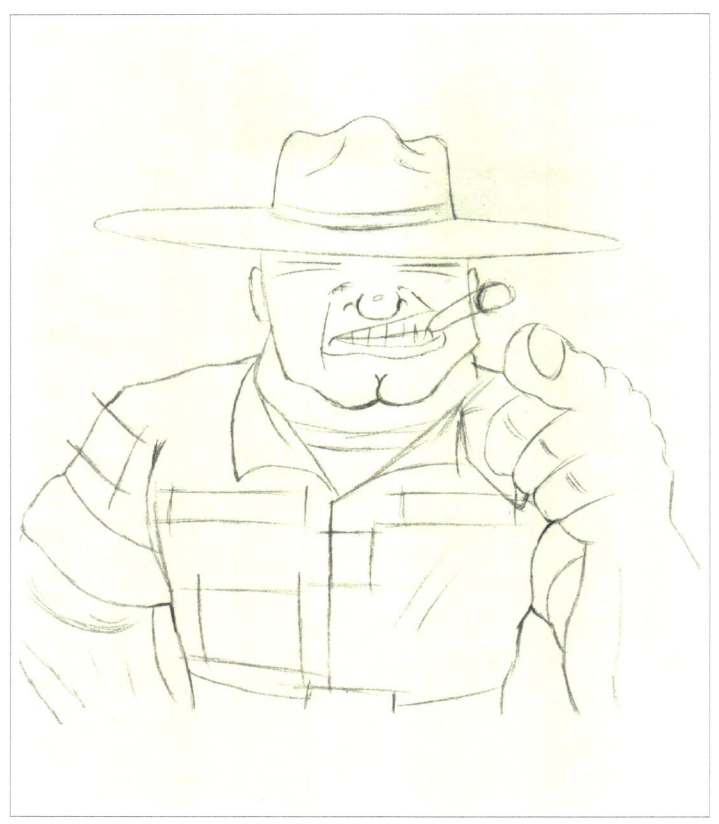

4. Next form the right hand by drawing the fingers. The fingers are bent to form a knuckle by drawing three sightly curved "V"s from the bottom left of the sketched pentagon shape. Connect the index finger to the knuckle from the first curved finger line. Distinguish the finger joints by drawing diagonal lines for each. Sketch the name tags/patches with broad long strokes. Finish up this stage by sketching out the cigar and sleeves on both sides of the arms

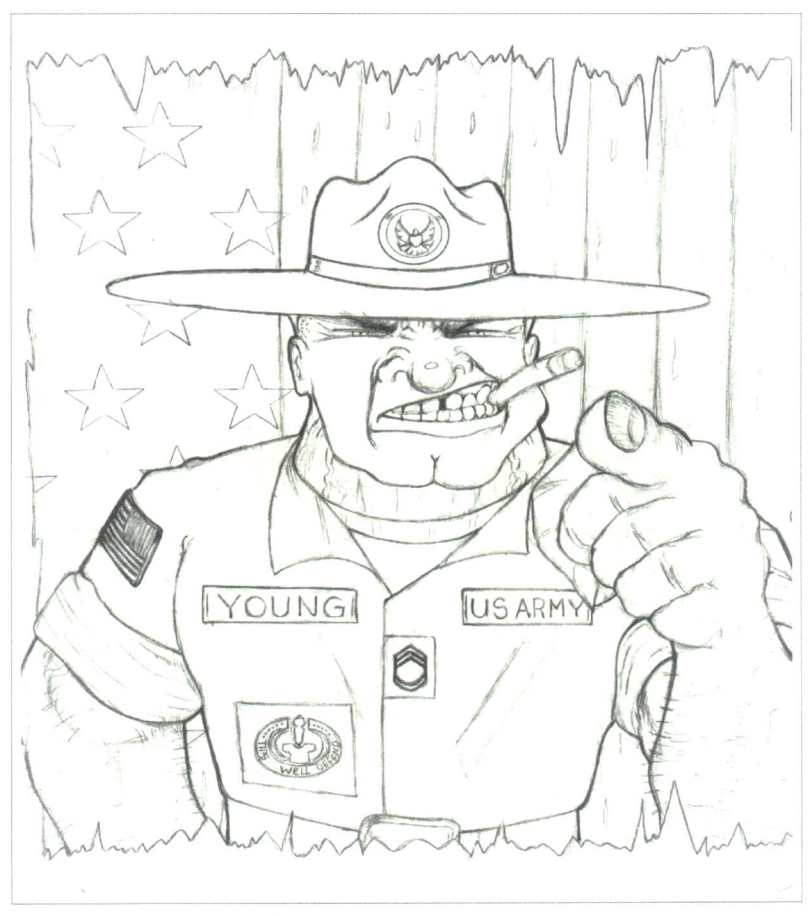

5. The final stage is the shading. Since I wasn't using an actual example, I had to improvise and imagine where shadows would fall on the drawing. I decide on a soft light from above this would allow me to bring out the seriousness in his eyes. When I shaded, I focused on less lit areas such as corners, areas under the hat or areas that converge and make hard intersections such as between the fingers, arms or creases in the uniform. Finally, one last critique. Clean up the drawing by erasing any stray marks and with that...

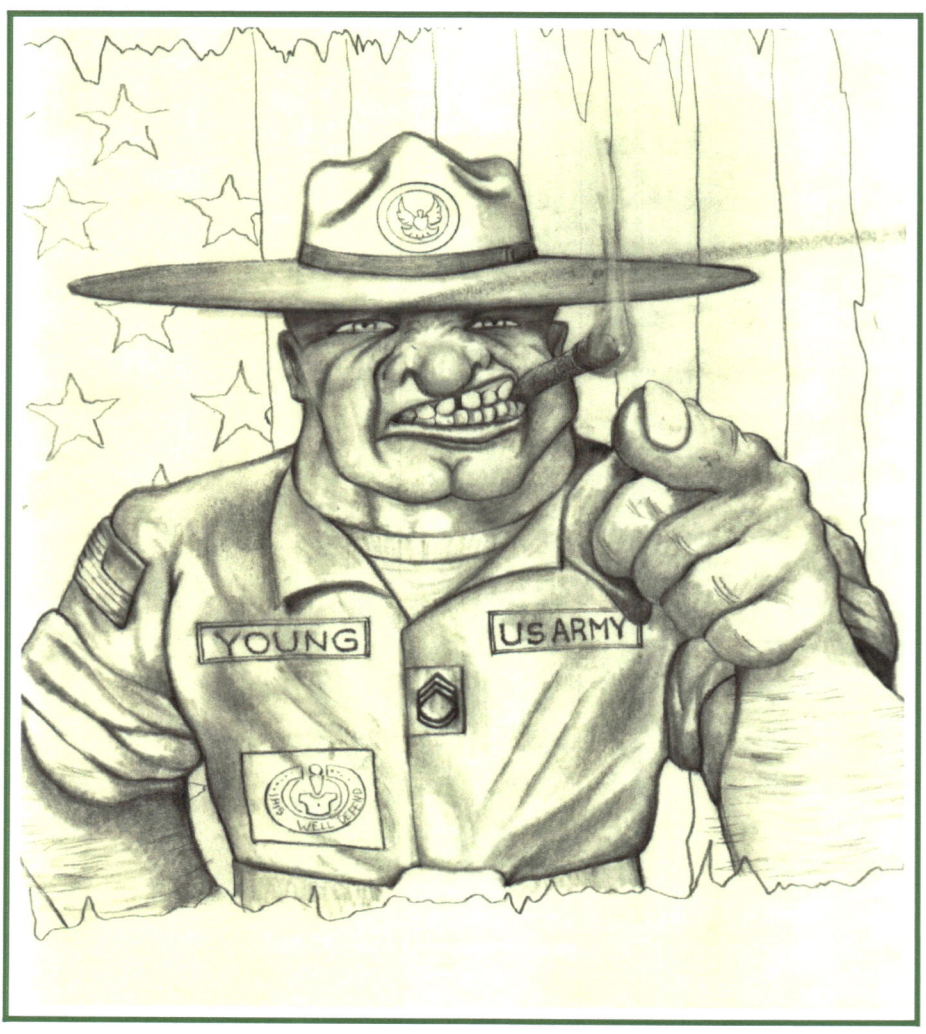

FINISHED PRODUCT

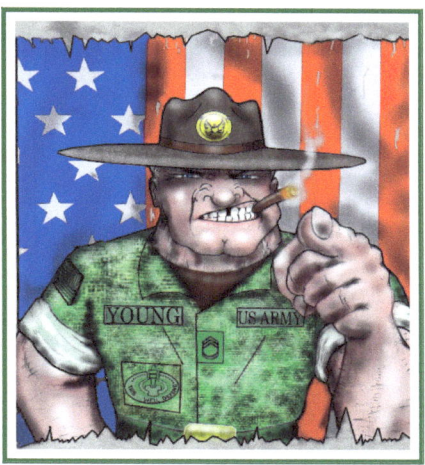 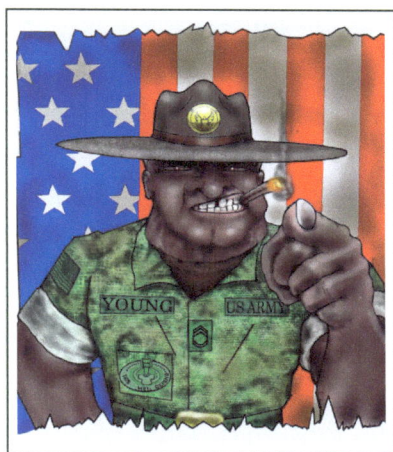

Cartoon Drawing Techniques

For not so technically perceptive individuals, (like me) it is better to use pencils because it is easier to make corrections without producing as many marks on papers as with the pen. Just like pencil, drawing, pencil line drawing techniques and shading produce excellent results.

Cartooning and Cartoon drawing refers to drawings that often have humorous and even satirical connotations printed on various media such as newspapers, magazines, and even the world of film. Cartoons may refer to animated cartoons, comic cartoons, editorial cartoons, gag cartoon and the illustrative cartoons

Cartoon drawings can be used for a wide range of purposes and media such as newspapers, comic books, comic strips, magazines, illustrations, film, as well as digital media. At it's most basic

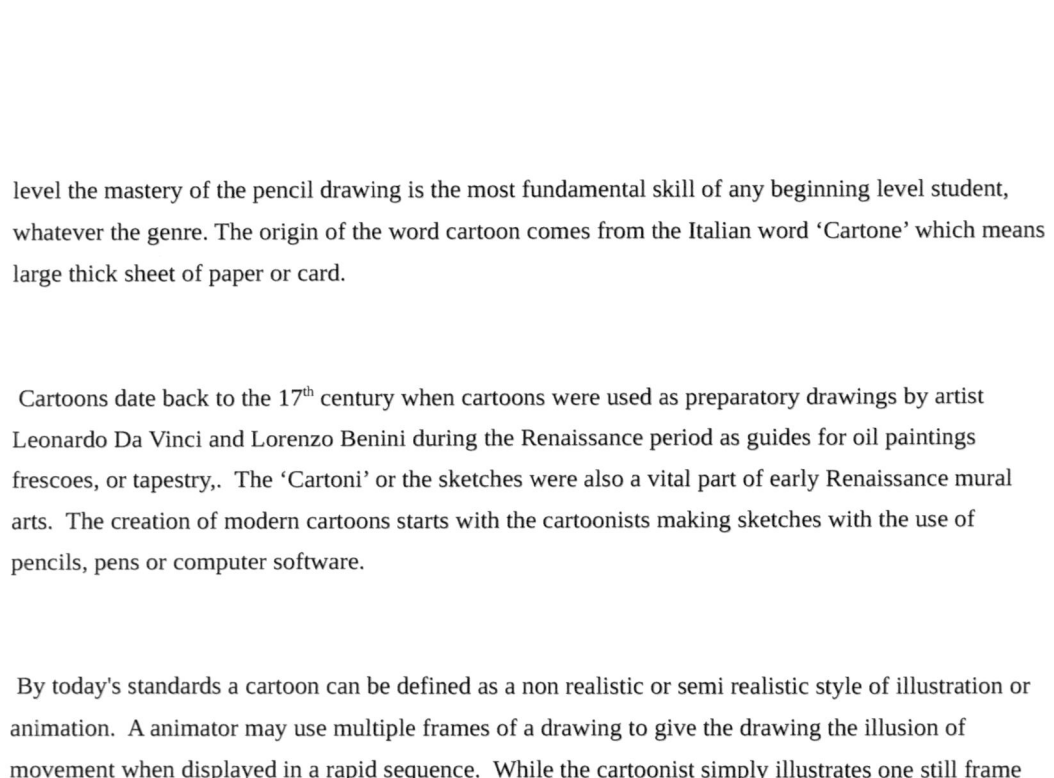

level the mastery of the pencil drawing is the most fundamental skill of any beginning level student, whatever the genre. The origin of the word cartoon comes from the Italian word 'Cartone' which means large thick sheet of paper or card.

Cartoons date back to the 17th century when cartoons were used as preparatory drawings by artist Leonardo Da Vinci and Lorenzo Benini during the Renaissance period as guides for oil paintings frescoes, or tapestry,. The 'Cartoni' or the sketches were also a vital part of early Renaissance mural arts. The creation of modern cartoons starts with the cartoonists making sketches with the use of pencils, pens or computer software.

By today's standards a cartoon can be defined as a non realistic or semi realistic style of illustration or animation. A animator may use multiple frames of a drawing to give the drawing the illusion of movement when displayed in a rapid sequence. While the cartoonist simply illustrates one still frame at a time. The cartoonist does work sequentially, however they use stagnant frames to tell the story event or get their point across to the audience.

Practice Exercise: #2

The Bulldog:

The Bull Dog will be much easier than the drill sergeant because we will be using reference material, a photo as a guide for the drawing. begin the drawing by defining size shape and form. This is done by lightly sketching boarder lines to gauge how close your drawing should extend in reference to the page. It helps by giving you a mental cue of generally where your sketch will be placed on the page. This will also assist you by helping you to center or frame the drawing on the page. It may not be a necessary step, but for the novice artist, these guide lines will help to simplify matters when staring from scratch.

REF PHOTO

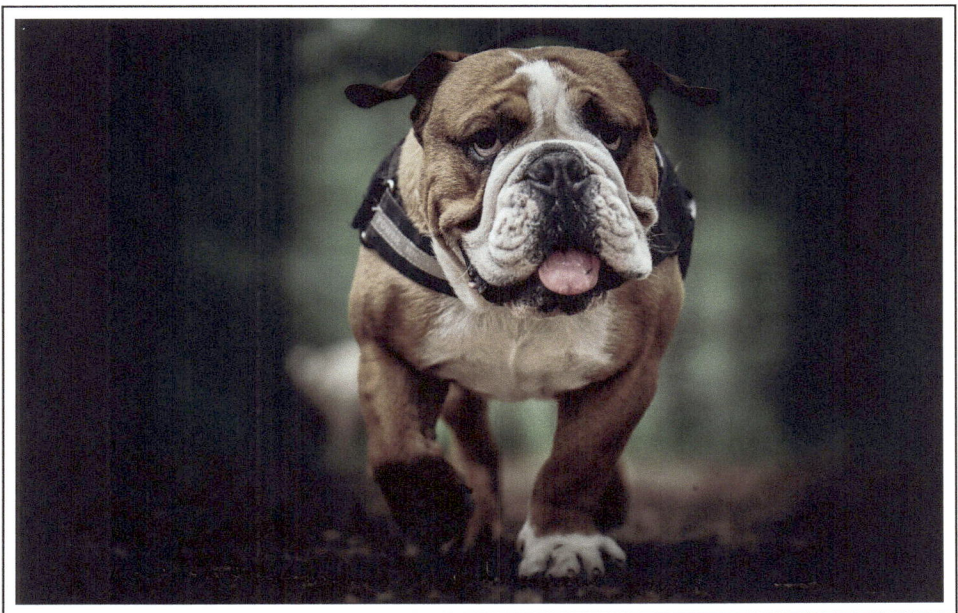

1. Carefully examine the reference photo don't just look at it, disassemble it, break it down into its most basic shapes. This will take imagination. Pay attention to small details such as how the head is tilted slightly to the left. The body of the bulldog can be a larger circle connected to the squarer head. Next from the circle sketch two parallel lines on the right slightly diagonal square off the bottom of the paw with a horizontal line. The left leg will be drawn from the larger circle also the joint nearest the foot will be cursed slightly inward to resemble a bend and continue the sketch with the hind legs from the main circle to the ground. Keep your hands and wrists loose. Note, the trailing paws will be slightly higher off the ground which is the affect of perspective on the dog, which we have discussed earlier in the book.

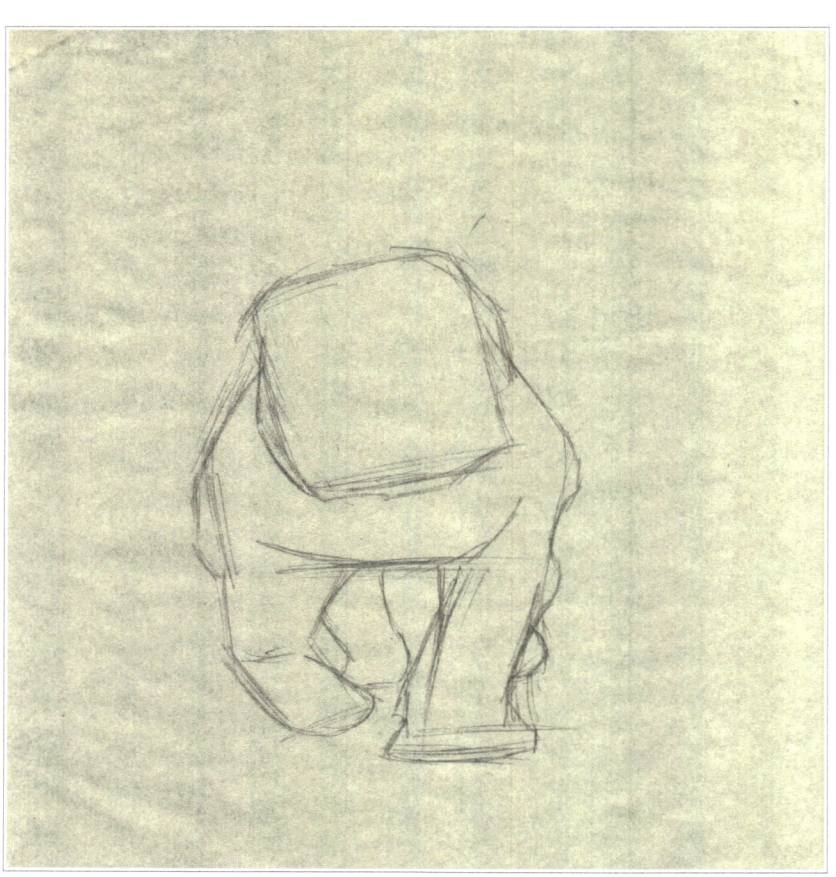

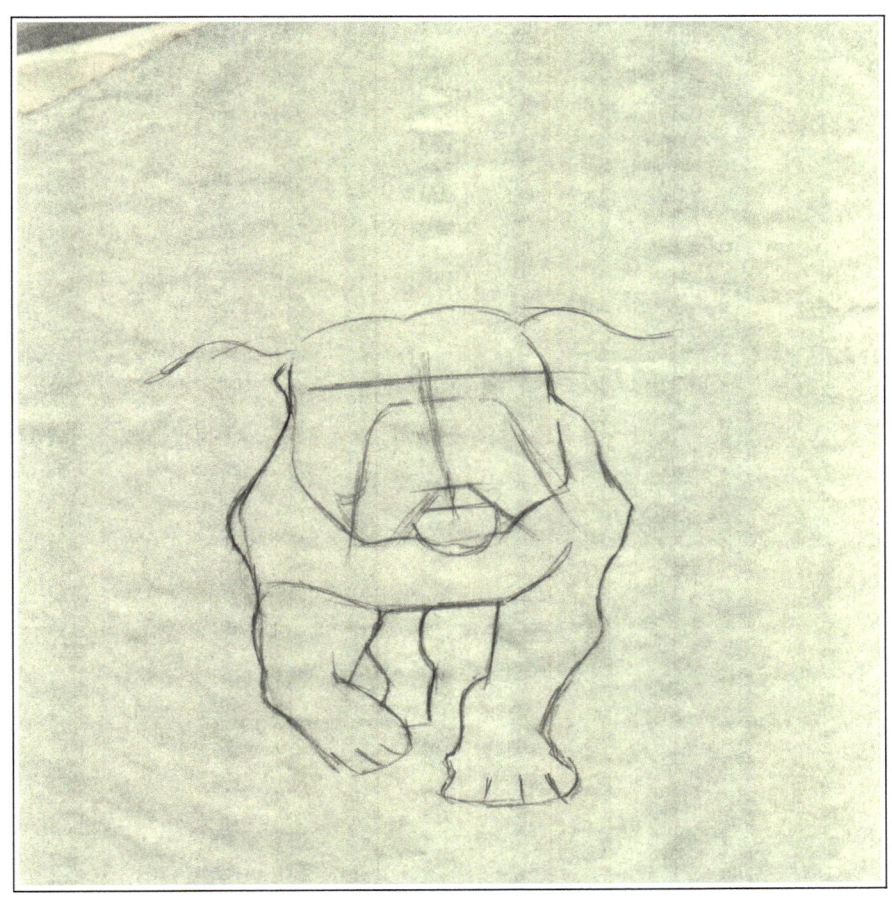

2. Begin to "carve" into your basic shapes and smooth the rough edges. Lightly sketch the mouth and eyes. The snout or nose is square shaped and will extend from the bottom of the jaw to 2/3 the distance of the head. The eyes will be roughly 1/5 from the top of the snout to the top of the head. The mouth should be centered using an imaginary line down the center of the head. Begin to shape the legs and toes following the contour lines of the reference photo. Divide the toes by sketching three evenly spaced lines on each leg. To form the mouth draw a triangle and the tongue will be a half circle, again all centered using your imaginary line.

3. Next form the ears by sketching curved and wavy lines as well as the top of the head. Shape the snout and lightly draw the nostrils. Continue to round and smooth out any hard edges such as around the mouth, tongue and continue to define the legs. Look at your reference material draw evaluate, erase if necessary. Look, sketch, evaluate, correct. This is the sequence that I use. (Similar to wash, rinse and repeat).

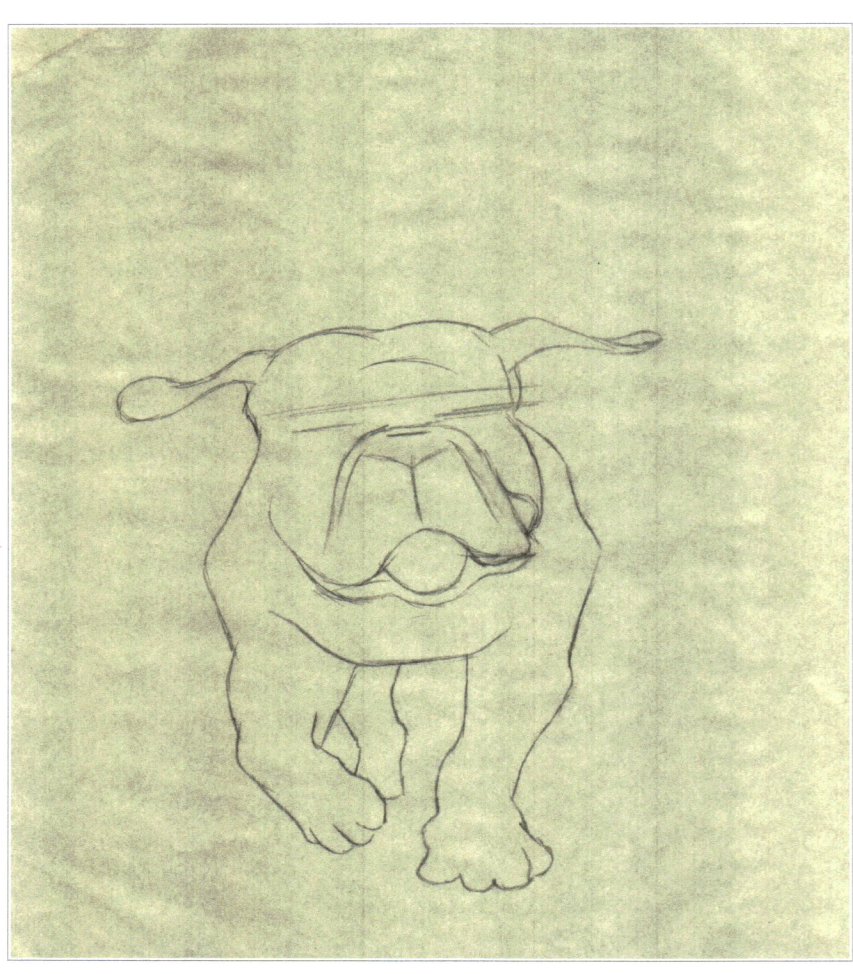

4. Continue to shape the drawing. The eye line should be horizontally divided into 5 brackets. The eye will be places inside the 4th and 2nd brackets.

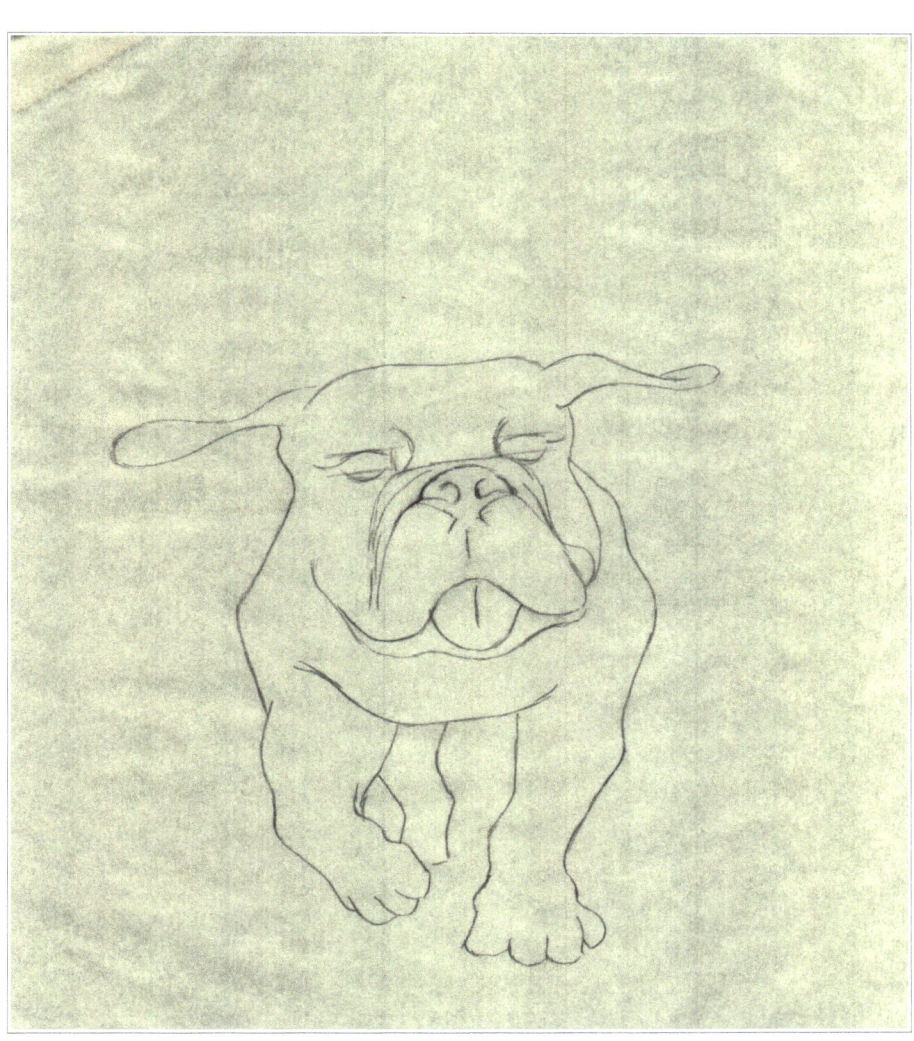

The eyes will be more rounded than human eyes. Shape the nose and the jowls as well as the chin. This will be your line drawing. At this point you can consider light sources and where shadows should fall. Look closely at your photograph or reference material as a guide for light and shadows.

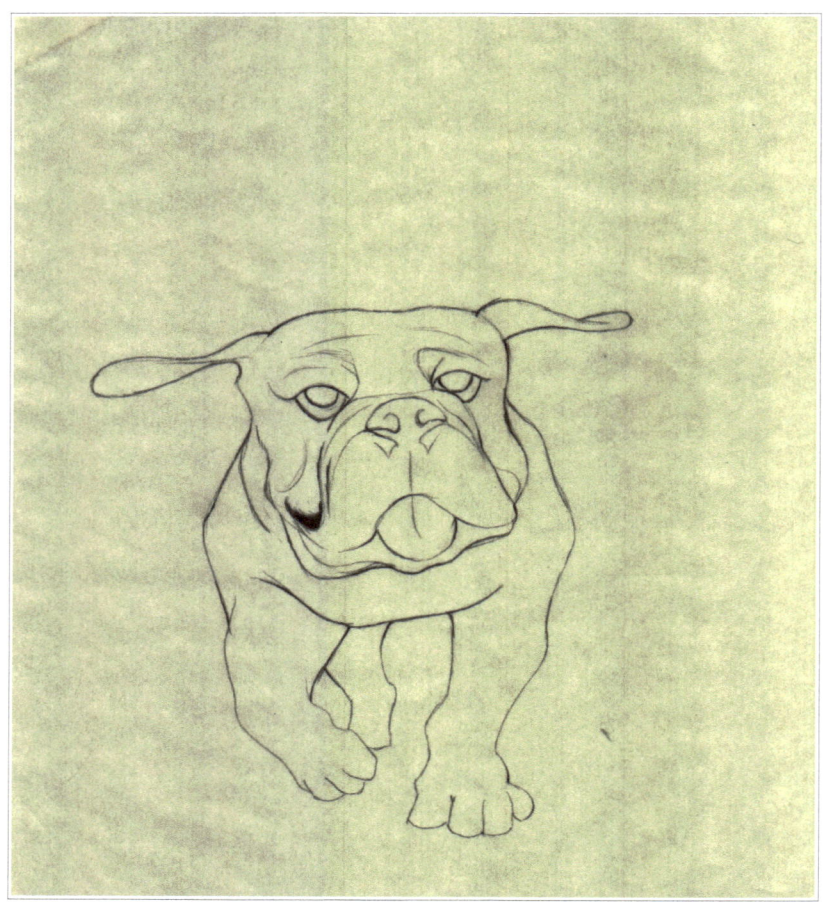

5. Finally the shading stage. So this is the final drawing. When you begin, use the pencil grade and harness that best fit the task you want to accomplish. For dark area the "B" for lighter the "H". Pay attention to the corners and how light placement determines where shadows will fall. Remember just

because the drawing appear to be white or black doesn't mean it is. It is only a lighter shade or grade of graphite on the paper. Use your cone blender, gradually blend areas. In some cases, the blender can be used as a substitute for the pencil by using the residual graphite that's left over on the tip of the stick. At this stage be careful not to smear your work. Pay attention to hand and arm placement. Frequently wash and clean your hands. You can also use a scrap piece of paper to cover areas you've shaded to avoid smearing or rubbing body oils into the paper. Finally one last critique. Erase if needed, brush and shake any residue off. At this point you may spray with a quality fixative to seal your work. It's ready for display.

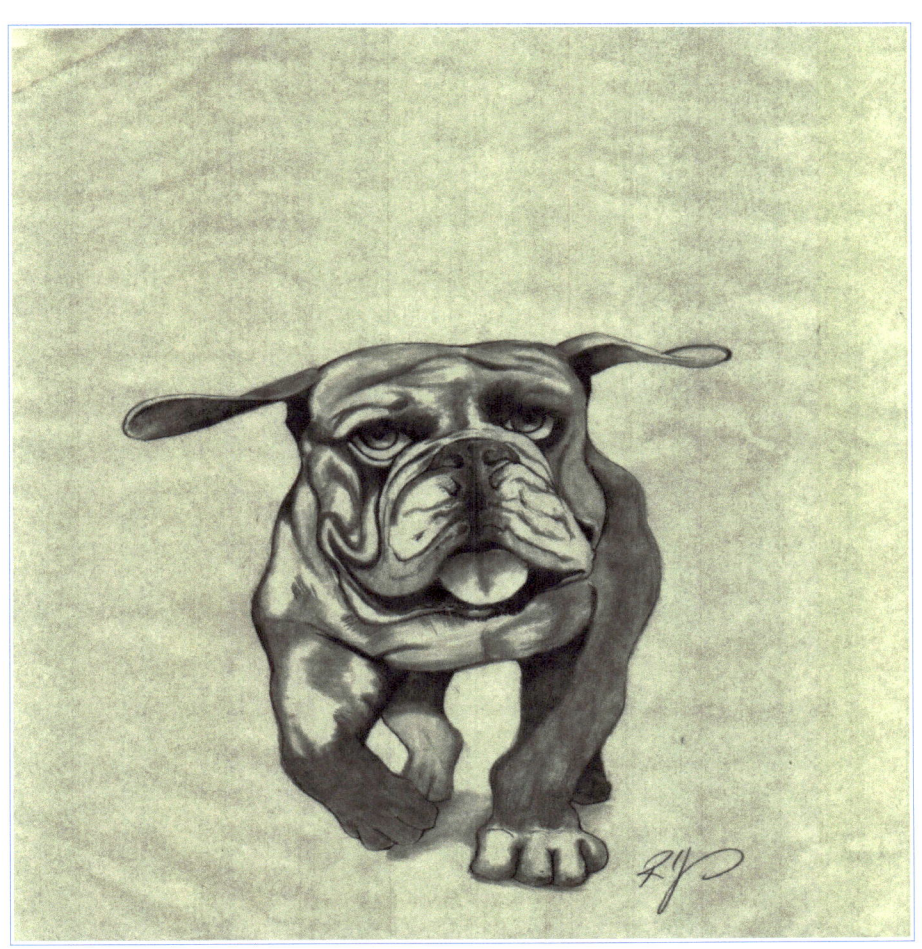

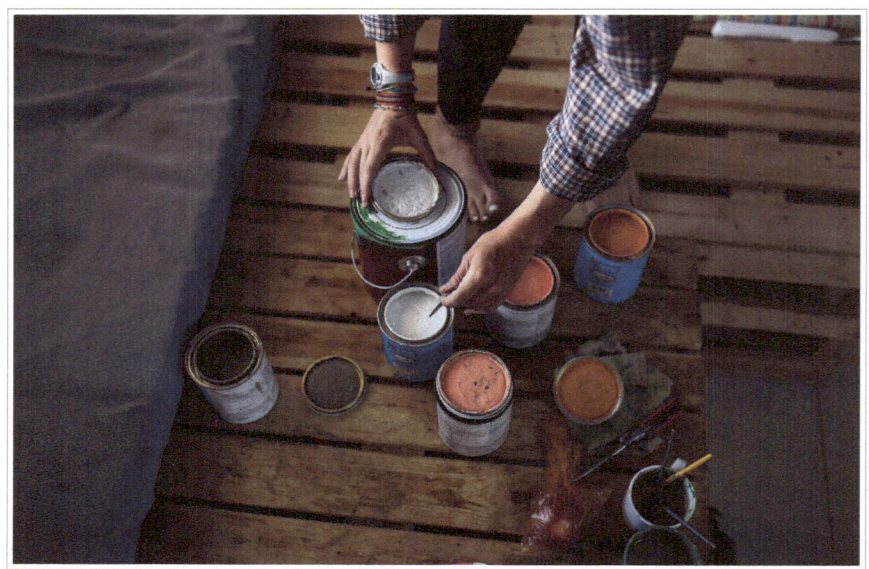

Pencil Drawing Can Help in Your Mural

Murals and wall paintings have its origins in early French and Mexican history where. The Muralista movement rose in popularity often being used as a social tool to educate the broad mass of people, with respect to political issues and trends through the art.

At present, wall paintings nowadays are gaining popularity in individual homes by transforming and adding a different mood and atmosphere to ordinary rooms and spaces. Wall paintings are common in nurseries, children's bedrooms, man caves, she sheds, or whatever one can imagine, all in the comfort of your home.

One of the basic characteristics of wall painting is its large size. Mural have an advantage and a dis advantage. On the one hand you may have a large space to work with, but on the other hand, that huge space may be hard to manage.

In fact, once you start painting on the wall without proper preparation, you may end up committing irreversible mistakes that require you to repaint. This is where pencil drawing comes to the rescue you from getting into this trouble.

Most wall painting commissions nowadays make use of the so-called drawing grids and pencil outlines on the walls before laying their paint brushes on these walls to save paint, materials, time, and to have more accuracy in their murals.

There are different ways of making grid lines for your wall painting. The more traditional one is by using a pencil and dividing the walls into grids. The more modern approach is with the use of projector by projecting a ready made grid unto the wall.

Most artists though prefer to use the traditional method, especially for outdoor wall paintings since the use of projector is quite expensive for long hours of use in a large painting endeavor. So, many artist use the projector method, although, basic rendering by pencil on the wall is much easier and faster.

Here is a systematic method of drawing the grids for your wall painting through pencil.

1. You need to conceptualize your design and how large is. Then, you need to scale the designs into grids with the use of a ruler to show how exactly it should appear on the wall note when scaling the drawing will need to be measured and scale to the wall for example 1 inch on the drawing will equal 1 foot on the wall sizes may vary. Before marking the wall make sure it is clean and is in a good state of repairs(no oil, dirt, grease, cracks, unwanted holes, birds nest, garden gnomes ect.)

2. Do the same thing on the wall by measuring and marking off the corresponding grids on the wall converting the smaller scales in your image to bigger squares on the wall. Here you would need a level to check if the lines, both vertical and horizontal, are
straight enough. Trick use a leveler with a straight edge

3. Try to mentally project and identify the grids of the small image with the larger grids on the wall. Start drawing the image on the large wall with the use of a pencil using correct hand and eye coordination.

4. Once you are able to draw the image on the wall, it is now time to erase the grid lines and use the pencil drawing remain as your painting guide, (similar to painting by numbers).

5. Paint your wall design with a fast drying acrylic paint and a flat brush making sure that you paint first the large areas. The details such as shading, blending, establishing shadow and tone will also be added later. This process again evolves critique, evaluation and patients, until you are satisfies with the results.

6. Allow your work to dry and settle,.you may even place a clear coat for protection.

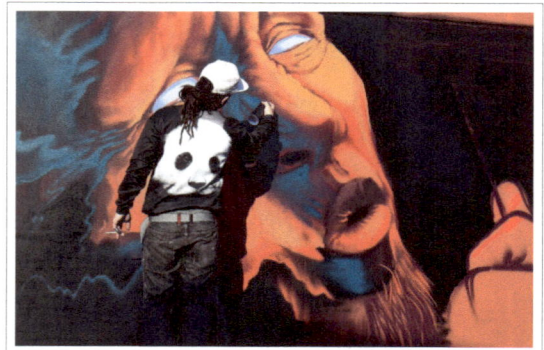
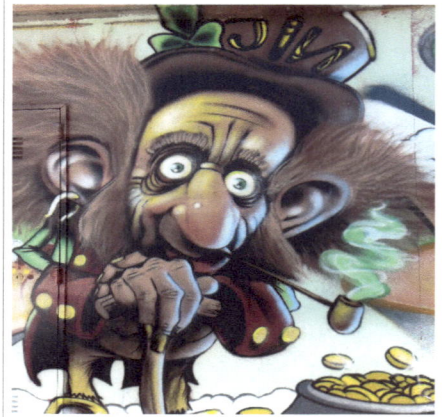

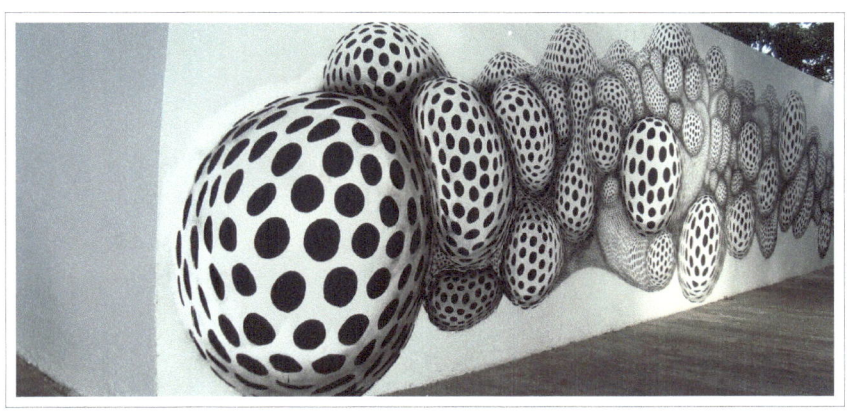

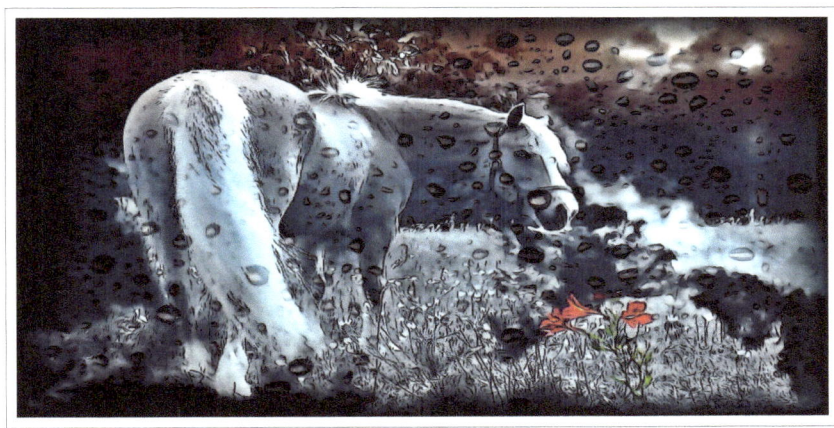

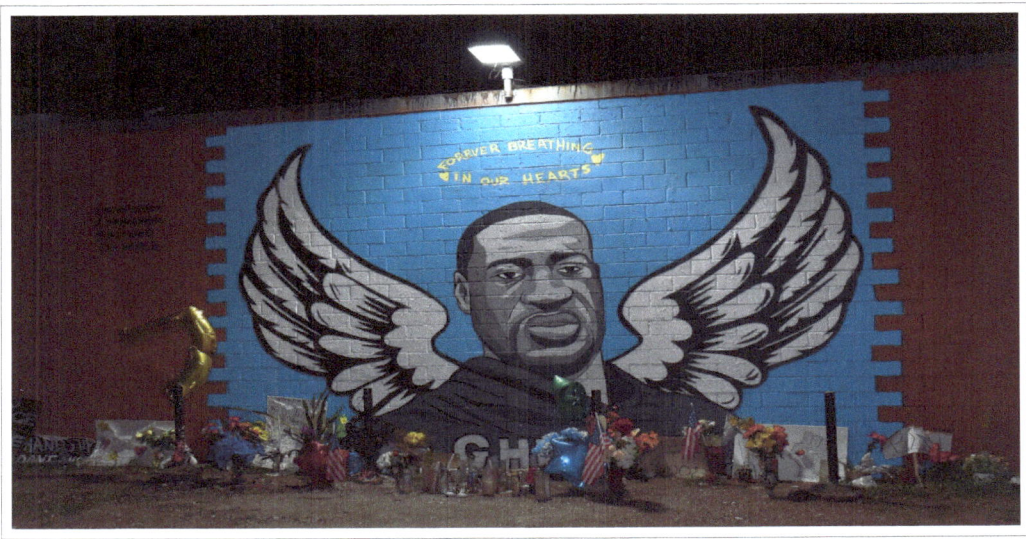

Conclusion

I hope you enjoyed this book and found the exercises useful. What we've discussed in this book are only the basics to success, but don't be discouraged if your work isn't perfect.

I can't stress it enough practice is the key. If you don't use it, you loose it. This requires time and effort. Draw what you see as well as what you don't. Dream, imagine, create and be creative. Art comes from the mind, body, and soul so don't hold back, you control the narrative, the sky's the limit with drawing.

Make a living selling your work, understand marketing. Get your work out there. Display it in art shows, social media, websites, and other sources. By definition it was drawn to seen shown off and admired.

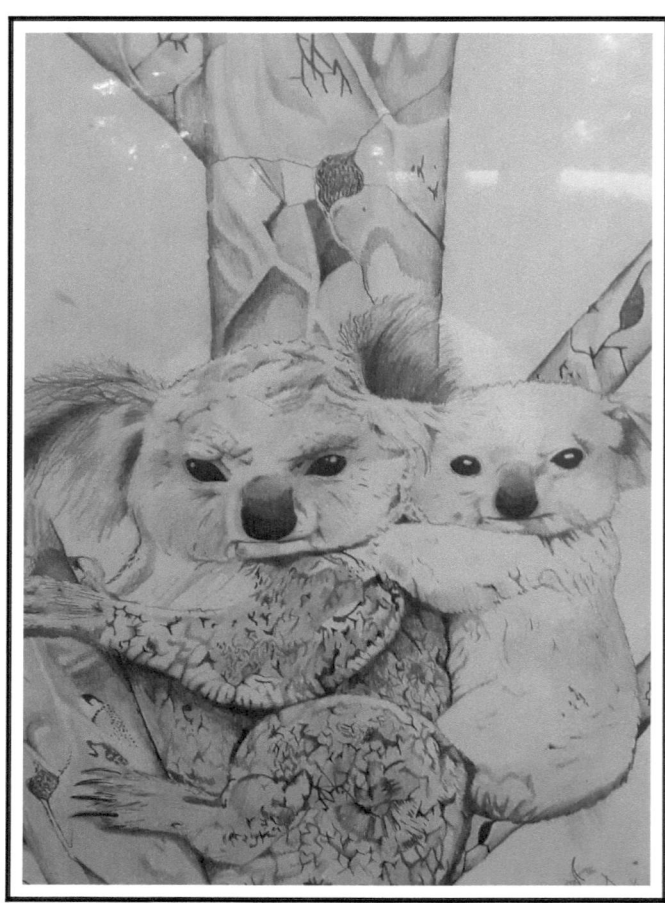

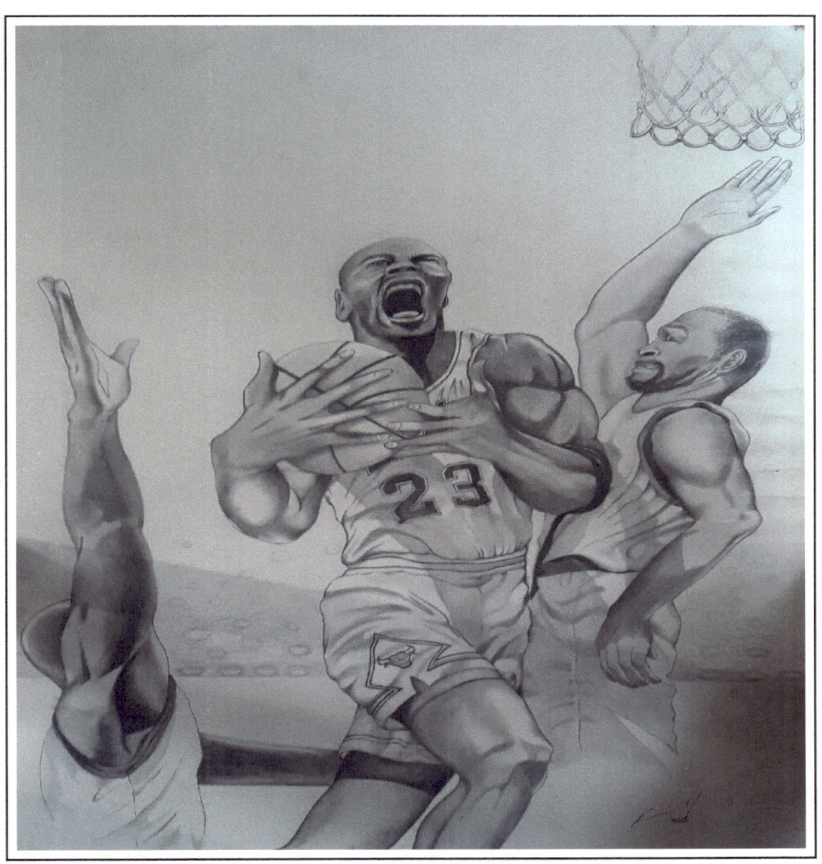

Expand, explore experiment with other fields such as watercolor, charcoal, mixed media, oil painting, airbrush digital art graphic design or murals and this is only the tip of the iceberg. Don't limit yourself to just one genre. Explore, get your feet wet and continue to build up your resume of work. With a little effort you will be successful. **Thank you, and good luck on your journey.**

R. K. YOUNG

For More of My Work, Visit Ripple Effect My New RedBubble Store At:

https://www.redbubble.com/people/ronnieyoung/shop?asc=u&ref=account-nav-dropdown

www.ingramcontent.com/pod-product-compliance
Lightning Source LLC
Chambersburg PA
CBHW040237220526
45473CB00001B/274